Penny Plain Twopence Coloured

THIS is the first complete history of what is known as the Juvenile Drama—the little toy stage with which children used to amuse themselves in Victorian days. Charles Dickens made frequent references to the pastime of colouring and cutting out the sheets of scenes and characters of such plays as "The Miller and His Men"—the classic of the Juvenile Drama—and Robert Louis Stevenson, in his well-known essay, "A Penny Plain and Twopence Coloured," extolled the plays of Skelt and Pollock. But Stevenson ignored the claims to fame of the real pioneers of the cardboard drama, among whom were such publishers as West, Hodgson, Jameson, Park, and Webb, whose early sheets of the plays were beautifully drawn by such artists as William Blake and George and Robert Cruikshank.

Mr Wilson, who succeeded Mr William Archer as dramatic critic of the London *Star*, has gone fully into the matter of the origin and development of the miniature stage of the Juvenile Drama, and has added appendices giving the publishers of the chief plays. The book contains a large number of fascinating illustrations and should interest all concerned with the stage and its history as well as artists, designers, and collectors and admirers of the quaint fads and fancies of Victorian days.

Mr C. B. Cochran, the famous producer, says in his Foreword: "This book was obviously wanted to fill a gap in the literature of the drama.... [It] has cast for me an unsuspected glamour on my childish pastimes and will give pleasure to many like myself who did not realize they had played with gold and precious jewels unawares."

A BACK SCENE IN "THE MILLER AND HIS MEN"
Drawn and engraved by W. Webb and coloured by his son.

Penny Plain
Two Pence Coloured

A History of the Juvenile Drama

By

A. E. Wilson

With a Foreword by

Charles B. Cochran

and Eighty-three Illustrations

George G. Harrap & Co. Ltd.
London   Bombay   Sydney

First published 1932
by GEORGE G. HARRAP *&* CO. LTD.
39-41 *Parker Street, Kingsway, London, W.C.*2

*To
Paul and Rodney*

Foreword

LET me say at the outset that I am quite unqualified to write a foreword to this book. Beyond Stevenson's " A Penny Plain and Twopence Coloured " and occasional references to the virtues of toy theatres by bright young critics who find our contemporary stage a bore, my knowledge of the history of the Juvenile Drama is non-existent, or rather was until I read Mr Wilson's interesting and informative study. This book was obviously wanted to fill a gap in the literature of the drama and now that Mr Wilson has done it, one wonders why it was never done before.

My own first-hand knowledge of the toy theatre is limited to the practical enjoyment of one, first, when I was a very little boy, and again, at about the age of sixteen, with my schoolfellow, Aubrey Beardsley.

I must have thrown away a fortune on my hobby. All my pocket-money in the early 'eighties went on sets of plays, and my father and mother were generous in contributions to the cost because the toy theatre kept me out of mischief!

But it was " The Miller and his Men " which stopped my ardour when I was about nine.

In working up the climax, with revolving mill, red fire, and so on, I felt the lack of four or more hands. Pushing on a character in a tin slide, lighting the red fire, manipulating a trap and working the wheel, while at the same time speaking the lines of the characters, made me lose my presence of mind.

The character in the tin slide caught fire, the flames spread to the wing; I burnt my hand, and then the great conflagration! My theatre was reduced to ashes.

I was always forbidden to use footlights by my mother, who in this showed an imagination well in advance of her time. A stage without footlights then seemed impossible to me, and, indeed, has seemed so to English producers as a whole years after. They have been dropped by advanced European and American *metteurs-en-scène*.

After the great fire, I finished with the toy theatre for seven years until I found myself sharing a study at school with Aubrey Beardsley. We disregarded the published ' sheets ' and the plays specially adapted for the purpose, staging instead dramas concocted by ourselves, with characters and scenery drawn and painted by Beardsley.

With the theory and history of the subject we were not concerned. We were practical men of the theatre, or so we thought ourselves!

I cannot remember any grown-ups playing with the toy theatre in my day, but many of my little friends at Brighton spent their pocket-money as I did at a little shop in North Street (east side). Ginnett's Circus (now the Grand Theatre) stood on the opposite side later on.

This shop sold nothing but toy theatres and their accessories.

I bought packets and packets of spangles, which were not sold for use on the big plates only. I made a very creditable transformation scene for " Jack and the Beanstalk " by sticking spangles on the plain scenes after I had coloured them. I stuck them, too, on little figures of harlequin and columbine with the richest effect.

There were other shops in Brighton where I could buy the sheets and characters, but the North Road shop was the only one which confined itself exclusively to the industry. There was even a shop in my native village of Lindfield, Sussex, where I could buy material.

I do not remember the names of any publishers of my favourite sheets other than Burtenshaw, and this sticks in my mind only because I had a school friend of the same name. Two of my favourite plays were " Sixteen-string Jack " and " Jack Sheppard."

My father, who was a great admirer of George Cruikshank, once told me, I remember, that some of the figures were designed by the famous caricaturist.

As a remote descendant of William Blake, I am excited to learn for the first time from this book that he designed some of my toys. Beardsley taught me to know Blake's work very well, but I do not think he can have known this either.

In the main, I agree with Mr Wilson that the pleasure of the toy theatre was in anticipation rather than in realization. I don't think I ever got through a performance of an entire play. Certainly, the audience never stayed right through from beginning to end!

This book has cast for me an unsuspected glamour on my childish pastimes and will give pleasure to many like myself who did not realize they had played with gold and precious jewels unawares.

CHARLES B. COCHRAN

Contents

Chapter One—Overture .... Page 13
Chapter Two—"Long-drawn Disenchantment" .... ,, 17
Chapter Three—Green the Inventor .... ,, 29
Chapter Four—Making the Play .... ,, 39
Chapter Five—Homage to Willy West .... ,, 45
Chapter Six—Hodgson, the Immortal Skelt, and Some Others .... ,, 51
Chapter Seven—Stevenson's "Poor Cuckoo" .... ,, 61
Chapter Eight—Magic in Hoxton .... ,, 69
Chapter Nine—Stage History in Miniature .... ,, 77
Chapter Ten—"The Miller and his Men" .... ,, 83
Chapter Eleven—The Book of the Play .... ,, 93
Chapter Twelve—Tinsel Portraits .... ,, 104
Appendices:
    A. Publishers .... ,, 109
    B. West's Plays .... ,, 111
Bibliography .... ,, 114
Index of People and Plays .... ,, 115

CHAPTER ONE

OVERTURE

We will draw the curtain and show you the picture.
                            Twelfth Night, Act I, Sc. v

WHY I have written this book is easily explained. My affection for the toy theatre of the real, old-fashioned kind—not your hideously lithographed, soulless, humourless, clumsy and ill-proportioned German production which is about the only thing of the kind that the toyshop now has to offer—dates from my early childhood when I first became the owner of a toy stage.

It is true that after the age of fourteen or so I ceased to be a proprietor and producer of the Juvenile Drama (to give it its classic and honoured name) and that my interest in the subject for many years afterwards may be said to have been academic—or at least less active. But no one who has ever possessed a toy theatre can lose entirely his interest in that little rectangular structure of wood and cardboard, with its neat row of tin footlights, its odd-looking orchestra, and its gaudily painted proscenium within which so

POLLOCK'S "ORCHESTRA STRIP"

many miracles of the imagination were attempted if not actually performed. My heart has always warmed toward the man who owned a toy stage in his youth; in him you will find one whose love for the real theatre is firmly implanted.

My own affection for the toy theatre has been abiding although it is many years since I parted with my property and ceased to lavish all my pocket money and such patience and skill as I possessed upon the fascinating task of preparing its plays. But I maintained an interest in it as a collector of the quaint " penny plain, twopence coloured " prints which have an artistic as well as an antiquarian and sentimental interest.

"How ignorantly they have been depreciated. How unjust, how foolish has been the scorn heaped upon the phrase 'penny plain, twopence coloured,'" once wrote Godfrey Turner, the dramatic critic who was a great admirer of the toy theatre and a notable authority upon its history.

Well, I for one have never depreciated it, and, as for heaping scorn upon that familiar phrase—why, for me it has always had a thrilling and stirring sound. In it there is an echo of far-off delight. Its very utterance evokes for me the vanished joys of boyhood and the magic of make-believe and conjures up, as few other things can, a glimpse of London of Dickensian days—the London as Cruikshank pictured it, seen perhaps through a golden haze which obscures all its imperfections and enhances all that it had of the sentimental and picturesque.

Some years ago while collecting the prints I sought to know more about the history of the Juvenile Drama. I wanted to know about its origin and who were the people who kept it flourishing for so many years. I inquired for a possible book upon the subject feeling sure that one must have been written. I found there was none to be had.

The *Encyclopædia Britannica,* devoting a great amount of space to nearly every other aspect of the theatre and to the most remote and obscure of subjects, had not one word to say about this most fascinating off-shoot of the British drama. The names of West, Hodgson, Jameson, Webb, and Pollock—aye, even that of the famous Skelt, were not even mentioned in any part of those comprehensive volumes. Books purporting to describe the toys of other days had nothing to say about the little toy theatre and its romantic associations. An incomprehensible omission! So it became necessary for me to write a book myself.

That a better book upon this subject could have been written any time during the past fifty years I readily and humbly acknowledge, but that those more competent than I have chosen to refrain from making any attempt at all is also true, and it is their neglect that has given me this opportunity. That is my sole excuse.

Robert Louis Stevenson, whose essay "A Penny Plain and Twopence Coloured" will be found to be a sort of King Charles's head in this book, at one time undoubtedly contemplated some such work. I do not know why he never carried out his intention, but of a certain check that he received while gathering material for the subject I have to tell elsewhere in these pages.

Another authority who could easily have written a history which for its facts alone would probably have put anything I could write completely in the shade was Ralph Thomas, a London lawyer whose splendid collection of sheets of the Juvenile Drama is now to be seen in the Prints Department of the British Museum. It is the finest and most complete collection of its kind available to the public and contains specimens of the work of nearly all the leading publishers of "theatrical sheets" as they were called.

Thomas was an ardent collector of these sheets of scenes and characters. Writing in *Notes and Queries* in August, 1908, he mentioned that he had collected since his boyhood 5,000 distinct prints published between 1811 and 1850. He had a thousand prints alone of Skelt's. Much of his collection was from that originally got together by Captain Frederick Hodgetts, "regardless of expense," as he says. For one copy alone of Hodgson's book of the words to "Guy Fawkes," originally published at fourpence, he is said to have paid £5.

It is to Thomas's contributions on the subject, ranging over a period from about 1869 to as recently as ten years ago, that I am greatly indebted for many of the facts contained in this book. Thomas had literary skill as well as a fund of knowledge about the Juvenile Drama, and he refers somewhere or other to the project for the completion of a history of it. It is a great pity that he never published it—if indeed he ever wrote it—because nowhere have I come upon one who knew more about the subject, who could discourse upon it with more interest, nor has there ever been one in his time who could have thrown more light upon the still obscure origin, early history and subsequent development of the toy theatre. In his day Thomas had known people like George Cruikshank, the artist, who had been actively connected with the business in its prime.

There are several collectors who could tell you much about the subject and all its associations. There is, in particular, Mr E. P. Prior who, though only a working man, as he is proud to confess, has a collection, the result of many years' devotion to a beloved hobby, which is the envy of all who have seen it. As a private collection it is probably unrivalled in the country. It contains many rareties and complete plays and sheets not to be found in the British Museum collection. All the great publishers are represented and he has specimens of most of their plays and books of words. To him I am also much indebted for information.

Another very valuable and interesting collection of everything connected with the Juvenile Drama is that owned by Mr H. J. Webb, the toy-theatre dealer, of 124 Old Street, E.C., whose little shop is a wonder house of quaint treasure. He is a living link with the famous Skelt, many of whose original plates he still possesses.

I have many times inspected the British Museum collection, which is contained in ten large volumes. To anyone interested in the subject they are a mine of information, fascination, and delight. The collection was the generous gift of Ralph Thomas, who would often come to the museum to inspect it after it had left his hands. The pictures are also of considerable artistic importance—far more so, in fact, than those acquainted only with the later and inferior specimens of the art probably imagine. There is also a complete collection of the Pollock (or Redington) publications in the Prints department of the Victoria and Albert Museum, South Kensington, the gift of Mrs Gabrielle Enthoven. In the little room devoted to "the art of the theatre" may be seen one of Pollock's toy stages fully set out with the scenes and characters of "The Silver Palace."

Apart from these pictorial records there is little to be found except in stray articles and essays in the theatrical and lay press extending over the past sixty years. In the past such people as William Archer, Godfrey Turner, John Oxenford, and John Ashton have discoursed most charmingly upon a congenial theme. Yet the sum total of the facts presented is little; their articles are to be read chiefly for the sake of their literary charm and for the spirit in which they were composed rather than for definite information upon the history of the subject. Indeed the majority of the articles—certainly the bulk of those that have appeared during the past twenty years or so—are full of inaccuracies and repetitions of one or two legends mostly about the Pollock business in Hoxton. The most recent article that I have read upon the subject repeated for the thousandth time the misstatement that Benjamin Pollock was the sole survivor in the business.

I have most agreeably spent my time in gathering the material for this book. Alas! I cannot claim that it is as complete a history of the Juvenile Drama as I could wish. So many of its notable purveyors have died in obscurity or have faded out of the picture leaving no trace of their history and activities—except such as can be gathered from the study of their sheets of characters and scenes—that material for a full record does not exist.

But here are brought together as many of the facts, dates, and names as I have been able to trace from many different sources and as many of the tributes to the charm and fascination of the Juvenile Drama as I have been able to find. I make no apology for this book being, like *Hamlet,* "deuced full of quotations." I have laboured over portfolios and files and dusty records, sometimes delving without the reward of a solitary new fact yet always repaid for my trouble by the charm of the old prints and by the delight of reading what other lovers of this fascinating old pursuit have had to say upon their pet theme. It really is surprising what an amount of graceful appreciation has been written. The stranger therefore the absence of any complete record of the subject of the toy theatre.

Let me add a note of thanks to all who have helped me in this pleasant task. I am particularly grateful to Mr Seymour Marks the Secretary of the British Model Theatre Guild (which has done much to foster an interest in the subject and in its later developments) for his kindly help and advice; to Mr E. P. Prior; to Mr H. W. Whanslaw of the London Marionette Theatre without whose help I could not have completed the necessary illustrations of the book; to Mr R. Crompton Rhodes, the dramatic critic of *The Birmingham Post,* for much information about the drama of the "penny plain, twopence coloured" period on which he is an acknowledged authority; to my colleague Mr F. W. Thomas for his friendly advice, and to Messrs B. Pollock and H. J. Webb whom I salute as the last survivors of a trade of particular charm and glory.

COVER FOR POLLOCK'S SCENES AND CHARACTERS FOR "LORD DARNLEY"

CHAPTER TWO

"LONG-DRAWN DISENCHANTMENT"

JUST about a hundred years ago the cult of the Juvenile Drama was at the height of its popularity in England. Now as a pastime it is practically dead. I doubt if any boy of to-day knows anything about the Juvenile Drama. Mention it to him and he will think you are talking about Punch and Judy, or the pantomime. Only in the rarest instance will anyone under the age of thirty know that you are referring to the little toy stage that once upon a time nearly every British boy used to possess and to those sheets of the play upon which he used to spend his pocket money.

"Penny plain, twopence coloured"—the phrase comes glibly enough to the tongue but there are many grown-ups who are ignorant as to its real origin and its proper application.

Well, part of the purpose of this book is to inform the ignorant about the toy drama, to communicate, if possible, some of the delight that it used to give, to arouse interest in its curious and little known history and, for those who once cultivated it as one of the hobbies of childhood, to recall some of the peculiar excitements that it once provided.

Never shall I forget that feeling of strange delight when some years ago I rediscovered after a long interval that classic of the toy theatre—"The Miller and his Men." As I handled the dimly but fondly remembered sheets of the play once again I recaptured for a moment some lost part of youth.

There they were once more—the old familiar characters in their odd, familiar attitudes. Grindoff (superb name!) with his right leg well outstretched and his left leg bent behind—the favourite stance of the cardboard Thespian—each hand grasping an enormous flintlock pistol, and all the rest of the fiercely-whiskered gang of robbers and their bland-visaged victims; the bandits 'carousing' in a solid indivisible mass around

GRINDOFF IN POLLOCK'S "THE MILLER AND HIS MEN"

"TIGHTLY-BREECHED SOLDIERY"
From Webb's "The Miller and his Men."

the oak table; the avenging and forbidding looking Ravina brandishing the torch; the nobly contoured, tightly-breeched soldiery with their neatly corked moustachios—wooden, sedate, as alike to each other as a row of peas.

And the peaceful looking mill and the homely cottage interiors, the castellated crags, the awesome cavern constructed out of Heaven knows what sort of rock formation and the landscapes that impressed one with the lavishness of Nature in Bohemia and the bold imagination of man!

I handled these old prints fondly and reverently, nearly dropping a tear of sentiment upon them. They seemed to me to have the substance of a dream. They evoked in me a precious memory of distant childhood—my first experience of the drama in any form.

BANDITS CAROUSING
From Pollock's "The Miller and his Men."

The performance took place in a dank and cobwebby old cellar, the chief illumination of which, I remember, was a bull's eye lantern. I, the entire audience, sat expectantly upon

THE AVENGING RAVINA
From Pollock's "The Miller and his Men."

an upturned ginger beer box, while my host, manager, and producer (aged thirteen years and many years my senior) staged for me a superb production of "The Miller and his Men," lavishing the entire pocket money for a week upon colza oil for the footlights and red fire in order to produce a really spectacular effect in the mill explosion scene which is the play's thrilling and overwhelming climax. Talk about a gala performance and a fascinated and appreciative audience! I was held rapt and enchanted by this truly magnificent drama.

I can only dimly recall the progress of the play and its procession of flat, highly-coloured, and rigid cardboard characters. I am sure I never completely followed its complicated plot. I can more clearly remember, however, the faint oddity of the fact that all the characters spoke with the same voice—my friend (the *deus ex machina*) tried in vain to capture something of Ravina's dulcet tones—and that awe began to dawn upon me when I first noted in the robbers' cavern the presence of a powder magazine which the producer had coloured a violent red in order to make it conspicuous against the background of sea-green rock.

But the impression of that explosion scene is still vivid. . . . I emerged from that dim cellar choked by the fumes of the coloured fire but thrilled to the core, a patron of the drama henceforth and the bond-slave for many years after of the toy theatre.

The Juvenile Drama must have so directed the minds of many boys irrevocably toward the stage. I know that it was the origin of my own passion for the theatre. It was my first glimpse of its enchanting mysteries and of the world of illusion.

Yet of course, although that was longer ago than I care to reckon, the Juvenile Drama had been practically extinct as a children's hobby for many years before I was born. However, thirty years or so ago one could still buy the penny plain, twopence coloured sheets at many of the old-fashioned toyshops in London and the provinces.

Particularly do I remember the lure of a little shop in that quaint and still old-world thoroughfare, Church Street, Stoke Newington. The sheets there had probably been long in stock for as I remember they were always a little faded and discoloured and faintly musty. To me that mustiness was the very odour of romance, the quintessential aroma of the Juvenile Drama.

Or in those days you could buy 'penny packets,' as they were called. They were ample and dreadful. An envelope vilely printed enclosed a giant sheet of the cheapest and coarsest paper containing the crudely printed reproduction of a stage front with accompanying orchestra and a few odd sheets of scenes and characters gathered higgledy-piggledy from all sorts of plays to fill in the blank places. How well I remember that one of the female characters was described as a " Roman pheasant," much to my bewilderment and incredulity. These sheets were cheap and nasty—the toy theatre alas! in its last stage of degeneration and decay, something that contained no hint of the real glory of the Juvenile Drama.

But if you bought the plays in sheets—Webb's and Pollock's—you could, for the modest outlay of a shilling or so, become the possessor of the real thing. It generally began, of course, with " The Miller and his Men " or perhaps with one of those queer and incomprehensible pantomimes with their Grimaldi-like clowns, sedate, long-skirted columbines, harlequins, pantaloons, strange policemen in top hats, and sprites, Jack Puddings, and goblins; glimpses of an odd-looking fairyland and of a harlequinade of a richer and more complex variety than we of our generation had ever experienced at Christmastide.

Then you hurried home as fast as your young legs would carry you to begin the delectable task of Preparing the Play.

You had, of course, first provided yourself with a stage with its quaint, early Victorian proscenium and its little row of tin footlights and the green-glazed calico curtain that was a constant anxiety, for you never knew when it was going up or coming down, or indeed whether it would ever move at all. But it was the preparation of the play and not the actual performance that gave one the intensest pleasure.

Ah, me, well I remember the ecstasy of it! The hours of glad toil with paint brush and water-colours, the glue and the cardboard, the glittering frost and tinsel paper for the pantomime scenes and the thick, rancid odour of colza oil which you burned in the footlights!

But let one who was more in touch with the pastime in its heyday hymn the rare joys experienced by the young producer and theatrical manager. It is John Oxenford, the eminent dramatic critic of *The Times* writing in *The Era Almanac* in 1871. He says:

> One of the great advantages pertaining to the toy theatre was the quantity of time that it occupied. The boy with his bare stage yet unprovided with proscenium and curtains, with his sheets of scenery and characters yet uncoloured, was supplied with ample employment for all the spare hours of the winter holidays. . . In my days the preparation for the performance gave infinitely more pleasure than the performance itself and the gift of a theatre with a piece that could be put into action at once would have been regarded with the indifference with which an angler would contemplate a basket of killed fish offered as a substitute for his expected day's sport. Even the purchase of coloured scenes and characters was deemed an effeminate occupation. Though he was nothing of a pictorial artist himself the boy of fourteen who could not do all the painting that was required for a moderately spectacular drama would have been looked upon as a very rare creature indeed.

A WEBB STAGE FRONT BEFORE CUTTING OUT
Showing "an elegant assembly of guests."

Yes, indeed, base and loathly was the boy who bought his sheets ready-coloured and sacrificed cravenly the joys of craftsmanship and the pride of creation.

If you have read Robert Louis Stevenson's essay "A Penny Plain and Twopence Coloured" (reprinted in *Memories and Portraits*) you may recall this charming passage:

> I cannot deny that joy attended the illumination; nor can I quite forget that child who, wilfully foregoing pleasure, stoops to 'twopence coloured.' . . . Yes, there was pleasure in the painting. But when all was painted it is needless to deny it, all was spoiled. You might, indeed, set up a scene or two to look at but to cut the figures out was simply sacrilege; nor could any child court the tedium, the worry and the long-drawn disenchantment of an actual performance. Two days after the purchase the honey had been sucked. Parents used to complain; they thought I had wearied of my play. It was not so: no more than a person can be said to have wearied of his dinner who leaves the bones and dishes; I had got the marrow and said grace.

"The long-drawn disenchantment of an actual performance." Alas! I am afraid that is the true description in the experience of most.

It is true that my first memory of a performance is of something powerfully effective and perfectly achieved, yet in the many years of devotion to the cardboard drama I cannot recall that I ever actually completed the production of or went through a whole performance of any play. One would say that there were tentative efforts, grand and promising beginnings, elaborate and even costly preparations—and then enthusiasm cooled. . . . One swept away the ruins and turned with a fresh zest to the preparation of another play.

It is, after all, the common experience. Goethe in his boyhood had a great passion for the puppet theatre. It entailed much about the same sort of preparation as the cardboard variety, which I am sure he must have loved if (as is quite likely) he ever saw it.

In *Wilhelm Meister* there is a long passage in which Wilhelm recounts to Mariana his delight in playing with his theatre puppets, and there he observes that the plays were never wholly represented, the performances being reserved "for the most part only for the fifth acts where the cutting and the stabbing lay."

He describes how he devoted his skill in cutting pasteboard and colouring figures to the work of preparation. Then he says: "You might have expected that henceforth one exhibition would follow close upon the heels of another; but it happened with me, as it often happens with children; they embrace wide plans, make mighty preparations, then a few trials and the whole undertaking is abandoned. I was guilty of that fault. My greatest pleasure lay in the inventive part and the employment of my fancy."

Yes, Goethe and Stevenson were right. The work of preparation was joy unalloyed but in my experience the business of stage-manager and producer was an affair mainly of vexations and frustrations.

There were those stolid, recalcitrant cardboard characters, moved on to the stage by too obtrusive tin slides, who simply refused to do one's bidding or to conform in the slightest to the emotions and passions supposed to be depicted in their parts. Those threatening bandits ever on the point of doing something desperate but always magnificently hesitant and inert! And those reluctant, hard-visaged bands of *coryphées* incredibly labelled " fairies dancing "! They were the problem and the crowning despair of the young producer.

FAIRIES DANCING

This was only one of what Charles Dickens in "A Christmas Tree" (*Reprinted Pieces*) calls "the besetting accidents and failures" of the toy theatre. And there was, as he described, that " unreasonable disposition of the respectable Kelmar (a character in ' The Miller and his Men ') to become faint in the legs and double up at exciting points in the drama."

There was a tendency too on the part of the characters, unless you were very careful, to topple forward and burn themselves to ashes in the row of footlights—a disaster involving the reprobation of parents and the grave warning about the possible revocation of one's theatrical licence.

Nor was the construction of the little stage itself without its attendant difficulties. I wonder how many juveniles ever tackled that ' built up ' front. It was a difficult job, complicated by the fact that certain essential guiding lines " marked A " and " marked B " were often missing from the paper proscenium. So unless you were highly-skilled and patient you compromised with a flat front.

That early Victorian stage front always fills me with delight. The boxes were filled with an elegant assembly of guests—stately, full-bosomed, matronly women with marvellously low *décolletage*, swathed in shawls, and dignified, bearded and whiskered gentlemen all preserving apparently a stoical indifference to the traffic of the stage. At least they were always gazing stolidly toward the audience.

There were separately printed pieces to form the orchestra. You could buy an ' orchestra strip ' for a halfpenny. The players were generally about three times the size of the spectators in the boxes and looked like Dickensian barbers, being marvellous hairy about the chin and extravagantly coiffured. To the eye of the musician the orchestra seemed oddly composed, consisting of a vast amount of wood wind and brass and a paucity of string. One admires the sturdy independence and indifference of a great number of the players who turned their backs to the conductor. One noted too how oddly the fiddlers handled their queerly-shaped instruments.

John Ashton in *Varia,* a collection of miscellaneous writings, has an article which seems to me to embody all the charm as well as to express all the tantalising drawbacks of the toy theatre. He says:

> These stages can now be purchased in toy shops but they are not the theatre of my youth; the occupants of the stage boxes who used to be dressed in the style of the dawn of the century are now modernized and are in consequence vapid to a degree whilst the very orchestras are tame and unenergetic and do not perform with the fervour of by-gone days. . . .
>
> These footlights were reservoirs for oil with six wicks requiring constant attention and trimming—a proceeding which they resented by emitting a most powerful odour of oil and dense black smoke which condensed into greasy smuts.
>
> Besides this brilliant illumination in front of the green glazed calico curtain there was a single wick-ed lamp placed on the side which brought into greater prominence the beauties architectural or arboreal of the wings; clouds hung from the top swaying in the most natural manner in every breeze whilst the scenes mounted on stout millboard were brought from the top through proper grooves.
>
> There were one or two trap doors but they were difficult to work and except in pantomimes were seldom required.
>
> The stage was provided with grooved slides for the reception of the characters but if used they provided an unnatural effect as, for instance, if William was on the same slide as Black-eyed Susan they must remain absolutely quiescent throughout the whole duologue because if William were to advance his Susan would retire precisely on the same ratio and William would be no nearer to his love.
>
> This drawback to the efficiency of the drama was obviated by having a number of independent tin slides with long wire handles by which means Susan might remain stationary or reciprocate William's advances and curvettings at the will of the stage manager. . . .
>
> Then there were set pieces such as 'Massaroni asleep,' 'brigands carousing,' etc. where no action was needed and these had little blocks of wood glued behind them and could be left to take care of themselves.

That able if rather austere dramatic critic, William Archer, while admiring the art of the Juvenile Drama had nothing much favourable to say of its actual performance. In *The Art Journal* in 1887 he wrote:

"The working of a toy stage is to this day a mystery to me. I never saw one in action and cannot conceive that any human soul could find pleasure in pasteboard performances."

Yet look at this further passage where he makes amends for this slighting criticism:

"It is precisely because performances never came off that the toy theatre is so infinitely preferable to its so-called real rival... It is the very gymnasium of the imagination."

And so it was. You were called upon to perform astounding feats of make-believe. Look at what this stage direction, gathered from the little book of words for the performance of "The Miller and his Men," says:

Exit KARL L.H. He is supposed to leave portmanteau off wing.

"Supposed," mark you, while all the time the stubborn pasteboard wretch would persist in clinging tightly to his irremovable property!

A little later in the same play one comes upon the direction "They bind his eyes." Zingari enter and the book of words curtly and unhelpfully says "The Zingari dance," leaving the bewildered young stage manager to decide how the miracle was to be accomplished. You could certainly not get the illusion by just jigging the tin slide containing the batch of stare-eyed, ringletted, and very sedate early Victorian ballet girls up and down.

And then there are such other exasperations as "KARL (shivering), "KARL (pretending to slip)," "LOTHAIR (aside)," to say nothing of such complicated stage effects as this:

Is about to fire in the air when Karl seizes him by the arm, the pistol explodes in the air, at the same time Karl stabs him with the sword. Take off table and figures quickly and put on Karl stabbing Riber pl 4, then take off R.H. and put on Riber dead, pl 4 Karl looking up at him pl 2 R. at the same time Friberg seizes Grindoff L.H. pl 4.

No, it simply could not be done with any satisfaction to those who sought for pure realism or desired to retain their reason.

"The actual performance," writes John Oxenford whom I have already quoted,

was not a very brilliant affair, the only persons really amused being the manager and his assistants, if he had any, so that yawns were frequent among the audience long before the final descent of the curtain. The dialogue read in a schoolboy voice became lamentably dull as the play proceeded and to fancy that it was uttered by any of those flat Liliputians who glided over the stage was beyond the power of the most unbridled imagination.

The characters sold in sheets of the present day are conceived with much more regard to completeness than those of olden time. To compensate for the absence of gesticulation the same personage is represented several times in different attitudes and a playbook composed expressly for miniature theatricals with short dialogues and long stage directions indicates the precise figure to be used in each particular situation.

In olden times, however, on the contrary, the framers of *dramatis personæ* were extremely capricious. Sometimes indeed they varied the attitudes of one person but very frequently he was

SIR LILLIPUT CARDBOARD WITH DRAWN SWORD

given in one position only and I have seen Sir Lilliput Cardboard glide through three acts of a serious drama with a drawn sword always ready to be plunged into the breast of an enemy whether that enemy was on the stage or behind the scenes.

The difficulty of giving lifelike movements to the figures has always proved an obstacle to the effectiveness of the toy theatre.

And apart from all these vexations and technical difficulties there was the question of expense. The upkeep of the toy theatre cast no small burden upon its juvenile owner. After you had bought your stage and the play there were so many extra items to provide for. There were such things as pantomime 'tricks,' land and water 'foot pieces,' rocks, tree trunks, and other odd items of extra scenery. Then if you were at all ambitious and hankered to make your transformation scene as gorgeous and as elaborate as the real thing you had to buy gauze for the transparencies, tinsel paper of various kinds, frosting, and spangles.

Then there were tin slides for the characters. If you wished the performance to go slickly you had to have a whole battery of these in readiness.

There was oil too for the footlights and perhaps candles or a bull's eye lantern for the lights in the wings. Lastly there was the cost of red fire—the most considerable of all expenses, for the Juvenile Drama commanded a lavish use of it for its most dramatic effects, and it went so quickly.

How many dramas depended for their culminating thrill upon this effect I know not, but such plays as demanded its use seem to me to have been constructed without regard for the purse of the young producer. "Red fire to burn"—there was a lavishness about that stage direction that urged one toward recklessness and bankruptcy.

But how ungenerous it is thus to dwell upon the limitations and defects of the toy theatre, a poor return for the hours of pleasure which it has given to me and has in the past given to so many thousands of children and, of course, to grown-ups.

At one time it might be said that the national pastime of the British child—at least in the winter—was the toy theatre. It was an absorbing recreation, the delight of countless evenings by the fireside.

Many eminent folk have confessed the pleasure they owed to the pursuit in their youth. Sir John Everett Millais, the painter, we read, was one of them; his father took a great interest in the painting of the scenes and helped his son to prepare the little plays for the stage.

Dickens was another, and many references to the toy theatre will be found in his books. Irving, Toole, Edward Terry, George R. Sims, Sydney Grundy, G. K. Chesterton—who once lamented that if he had not wasted his time in writing books and articles he might have been the greatest toy-theatre maker in the world—W. P. Frith, R.A., Robert Blatchford, and Gordon Craig have all described the pleasure they have derived from the toy theatre. It was Gordon Craig who once wrote: " In England we possess the best of toy theatres and the worst of grown-up ones. We consider Pollock's theatre as the very best toy theatre in the world and that Beerbohm Tree's theatre is the worst grown-up theatre in the world." Which if very unkind to Tree was at least very handsome to the toy theatre.

One of the most illustrious of those living who, in their youth, were devotees is Mr Winston Churchill. I had the curiosity to write to him on the matter and he was good enough to send me the following letter:

Chartwell, Westerham,
Kent

Dear Sir,

    I certainly remember visiting Mr Webb of Old Street, E.C. or some other shop of that kind in the neighbourhood and also purchasing from him from time to time some of his plays. The one I remember best is " The Miller and his Men." For three or four years of my life a model theatre was a great amusement to me.

Yours truly,
WINSTON CHURCHILL

And although it was more essentially a masculine pastime there were women devotees too. One of them was Ellen Terry who in *The Mask* in 1912 made the following charming acknowledgment:

> I remember the little toy theatres well and there is nothing quite like them. I had one when I was a child and they were known as Redington's theatres. I have no interest in the German toy stages which to-day are sometimes offered us in place of the fine old English toys. They cannot in any way be compared.

Some of these, of course—Mr Churchill and Mr Chesterton among them—were lovers of the Juvenile Drama in the period of its decline, or indeed when for the greater part of childhood it was practically extinct.

For I think as a juvenile pastime it expired somewhere about the mid-seventies. Even as far back as 1871 John Oxenford was lamenting its decay. He wrote:

> Although new theatres aristocratic and plebeian are springing up all over London and more money is laid out upon dramatic entertainment than in any previous period I doubt if Young

England feels the same interest in stage plays as the lads who flourished say forty-five years ago.

A small stage on which dramas could be acted by pasteboard performers with wings that changed by mechanical means and a sliding trap-door at the back was at the time of which I am speaking a most valued treasure a boy in his early teens could possess. The little stage was regarded as something above a mere toy and its management was deemed neither a childish nor effeminate pursuit.

The rise and fall of the Juvenile Drama indeed was one of the most curious and interesting features in the history of the English theatre in the early half of the nineteenth century.

It is difficult to believe that at the height of its popularity, between 1830 and 1840, nearly fifty firms were engaged in the trade and that many hundreds of people were employed in the various processes of manufacture, distribution, and sale. From a business point of view the trade was of no small importance though children appear to have been its main supporters.

Even in 1890 Kelly's *London Directory* contained not one entry under the heading 'theatrical stationers' although there were probably at that time a few firms still in business. Certainly there were the shops of Pollock and Webb, which still exist in the Hoxton district. But the omission shows that by that time a once important trade was no longer regarded as worthy of special mention.

The dramas, pantomimes, and other productions of the toy theatre had at one time a great vogue in America, which does not appear, by the way, ever to have produced a publisher of its own. According to the late John Bouvé Clapp, writing in the Boston *Evening Transcript* of February 6, 1915: "Nearly fifty years ago there was a store in Washington Street (Boston) kept by Salome where an assortment of these plays could be obtained." A few years ago a toy theatre exhibition in New York attracted a good deal of attention.

Except for the small demand made upon it by collectors, a few stage designers and writers, and those with artistic or antiquarian tastes, popular interest in the business is now practically dead, and what trade there is in the prints and little stages is confined to the two dealers I have mentioned. I doubt if it is possible to obtain anything in this line elsewhere in the country. I have made inquiries myself at many toy shops only to be told that supplies could be obtained only to order.

I have no doubt, though, that in many an odd corner or lumber room and in cellars up and down the country you will find these faded and forgotten relics of the glorious days —old stages, cut out characters and scenes of plays—the history in miniature of half a century of the British theatre in dim and discoloured sheets and scraps of cardboard.

The high-minded collector of theatrical prints may be scornfully superior to the suggestion that there is a commercial aspect of the Juvenile Drama. Nevertheless it is a fact that the value of many of these halfpenny and penny sheets has enormously increased and that apart from their artistic, sentimental and antiquarian interest they may be regarded as a very promising investment.

I do not think that there is a very active market in the older prints. Certain of them like those of West's, Hodgson's, and Jameson's are rarely to be obtained nowadays and it is therefore difficult to suggest what is their real value.

A set of four pictures of Mme Vestris, the famous actress of the old Olympic, originally sold at a halfpenny, once realised four guineas. Even later productions like those of Skelt, who turned them out wholesale, have fetched very high prices. Over thirty years ago Skelt's " The Miller and his Men," accompanied by the book of the play, was sold for four pounds and the buyer congratulated himself on obtaining a great bargain. Another set a year or two later went for five guineas.

A collector known to me has paid as much as fifteen shillings for a single plain sheet of Skelt's in order to complete the play and would be willing to give more for other missing sheets. It is still possible, I believe, to buy some of Skelt's and Green's plays for ten shillings and one pound the set, and one or two of Park's are procurable for thirty shillings or so. There is no doubt that the value of these plays will increase considerably as time goes on.

In contrast to these high prices I have heard of 'finds' that are enough to make the collector's mouth water. An old portfolio picked up a few years ago at a second-hand dealer's shop in one of the London suburbs for five shillings was found to contain rich examples of the production of nearly all the famous dealers from West onward and was in itself a handsome and representative collection of the Juvenile Drama. Recently a friend of mine unearthed a rich store of prints representative of most of the leading publishers. The duplicate sheets alone realised for him far more than he had given for the entire collection.

WEST'S CHARACTERS IN "THE LADY OF THE LAKE"
Dated August 5, 1811.
From the British Museum Collection

CHAPTER THREE

GREEN THE INVENTOR

MYSTERY, misapprehension, and mis-statement exist as to the invention and precise origin of the Juvenile Drama. No one knows exactly when it was first created, no one knows definitely who invented it, no one seems to possess the first sheet that was engraved. The encyclopædias are silent on the subject; you may look in vain in the *Britannica* for any mention of the Juvenile Drama or those associated with it in its history.

The misapprehension is in the minds of those who have read only a few articles by writers who have only casually studied the subject. The mis-statements are legion. I have even seen it asserted that Skelt was the inventor—Skelt, the prolific producer of other people's work, who came into the business long after it was started, who began by selling other people's productions, who did not design his own sheets and never drew a line himself! This particular mis-statement, I believe, has even appeared in a dictionary of biography and it is fostered among the uninformed by Stevenson in his picturesque glorification of "Skeltery."

We can narrow things down and declare with some certainty, however, that the inventor of the toy theatre scenes and characters, or perhaps, more correctly, the introducer of the idea into England, was either J. K. Green, William West, or R. Lloyd, and the evidence is strongly in favour of Green.

West, of course, has had his strong supporters primarily because some of the earliest prints to be found in the British Museum collection and in the hands of private collectors are his. An article by William Archer which appeared in *The Art Journal* in 1887 has had a great deal to do with encouraging this belief. As a matter of fact, Archer obtained the material for his article from a collector of West's prints, which considerably detracts from the value of his authority.

West was certainly a pioneer; he was a prolific producer; he engaged real artists for his productions, and he published some of the most admirable sheets known—yet there is no evidence that he was first in the field. His first recorded publication is "The Peasant Boy," dated February 26, 1811.

The earliest sheet in the British Museum collection is West's "The Council of Ten or the Lake of the Grotto," dated July 30, 1811, but there are also in existence sheets of the same year published by Jameson as well as others by Green and Burtenshaw, who published for Green. In 1812 many other firms were publishing; the business by that time appears to have been well on its legs.

Green himself claims to have invented the prints in 1808 though there are no sheets of that year in existence. On some of his prints, which were undated, appear the words "The original inventor," but we have no definite evidence as to the justice of that claim. I cannot, however, trace any attempt by any other publisher to dispute the claim very actively. That is rather an important point in Green's favour.

In any case, Green must have been very young at the time when he began publishing. He was born in 1790, so that even if he published no earlier than 1811 he was at that time only twenty-one years of age.

Mr E. P. Prior, who has one of the finest collections of these prints and may be regarded as one of the leading authorities on the subject, has gone very thoroughly into the question of Green's claim, and is convinced that he was the original publisher. He is still investigating and trying to trace the prints back earlier than the year 1811. I do not think that the question will ever be placed absolutely beyond dispute, but for myself I am satisfied by Mr Prior's statement and by the evidence of other experts whom I have consulted that Green was the man.

That confusion exists is explained by the fact that Green had some early business associations with West. His name appears on some of West's sheets, but in what capacity he served him is not clear.

The most astonishing thing is that though he was first in the field he outlived most of the rival founders of toy theatre firms.

Yes, Green who began, as there is some reason to believe, as early as 1808, was in the business until his death in 1860! It is an astonishing record and it entitles the name of Green in association with the Juvenile Drama to more respect and attention. Indeed, it has been the custom either to ignore his claim or to pass him by with the briefest of references. This is another of those injustices with which the history of the toy theatre appears to teem. I have read innumerable articles on the subject in which the name of Green is not even mentioned.

Yet Green had one of the most extensive repertories of plays, and it is a fact that the bulk of Redington's (now Pollock's) publications were his, only the name being altered on the plates.

Green appears to have been apprenticed to the printing and engraving trade and I think it more than likely that he himself drew some of his own plates.

What I believe is the earliest plate of his now in existence is dated May 1812. The play was "The Secret Mine" and you will find specimen sheets of it preserved in the British Museum Print Room. His early plates were poorly drawn and compare

ONE OF THE EARLIEST KNOWN SHEETS
West's "The Council of Ten, or the Lake of the Grotto." Dated July 30, 1811.
From the British Museum Collection

ANOTHER EARLY SHEET
West's Characters in "Macbeth." Dated July 31, 1811.
From the British Museum Collection

ONE OF GREEN'S EARLY SHEETS
Dated July 2, 1812.
From the British Museum Collection

ONE OF GREEN'S SCENES TO SERVE FOR A VARIETY OF PLAYS
Dated April 30, 1836.

very unfavourably with the work of West and Hodgson. The line work was hesitant and scratchy and the whole play was the obvious work of a 'prentice hand. "The Secret Mine" was boldly pirated from West's edition of the play, as may be seen by comparing the pictures which are here reproduced. Green's copy differs from West's original only in the smallest detail. His sheet bears an earlier date than that of West but it is probable that the latter was a re-issue or 'second edition.'

In the same year Green published "Seven Wonders of the World, or Harlequin Colossus" which was also inferior work. In 1814 he appears to have been working in partnership; at least "The Tiger's Horde," a crude-looking production which was published in September, bears the inscription "Green and Slee, theatrical print warehouse, 5, Artillery Lane, Bishopsgate."

And then he appears to have vanished—it is not known how or why—and he does not appear again in the business as a toy-theatre publisher until about 1832—some twenty years later. What became of him? One story—and I give it with reserve because it has never been confirmed—is that he was transported for pirating the work of other publishers. This may, of course, be only presumption, but the period of nearly twenty years is rather significant.

Anyway, directly after his reappearance there is a burst of productive activity in the way of "halfpenny plain" sheets which makes the Green collection one of the most noteworthy in its variety of choice.

In 1834 there was "Lord Darnley," "Rookwood," "Jack the Giant Killer"; in 1836, "The Brigand," "Children of the Wood," "Maid of the Inn," "The Forty

STIRRING TABLEAU IN GREEN'S "THE BATTLE OF WATERLOO"

Thieves," "The Ride to York," "Aladdin," "Harlequin Robin Hood"; in 1837, "Jack Sheppard," "Therese," "The Lord Mayor's Fool," "Wreck Ashore"; in 1840, "The Forest of Bondy," "The Waterman"; in 1842, "Black-eyed Susan"; in 1843, "The Battle of Waterloo"; in 1847, "The Flying Dutchman"; in 1852,

"Harlequin Oliver Cromwell"; in 1853, "Whittington and His Cat"; in 1854, "The Life of a Soldier" and "The Battle of the Alma," and in 1857, "Sixteen String Jack."

These, of course, were only his principal plays. A good many are in the Pollock collection and can still be obtained. The drawing in them, considering the low price at which they were sold, reaches a fairly good, competent level. In some of the battle pictures the draughtsmanship is spirited, though in many of the plays the characters are rather wooden and stereotyped. They lack freedom and individuality of style. Most of the figures are on the dumpy side, and for quite a long period they were evidently the work of the same artist.

The drawing did not improve as time went on and the standard of work published in the late forties and the fifties was considerably below that of the thirties, although some of the scenes are not so bad. There is a monotony about the drawing of the forest pictures and the luxuriant foliage with which Green's plays abound and some land and seascapes are positively amateurish.

"Green's 'Jack Sheppard,'" writes Theo Arthur in *The Era* Almanac (1891), "beats every other play published for the number of sheets of characters and scenes that it required in its fullness—some fabulous number it was—which the savings of no ordinary pocket money could ever hope to procure; it required a rich uncle (after dinner) or a godfather in a good humour to finance the youthful manager for the drama in question."

Another curiosity about Green's business is that it rarely appears to have been directly conducted by him. He seems to have disposed of all his prints through the agency of dealers. Thus we find a diversity of addresses upon his sheets which must have been those of his private residences. His productions were mostly sold wholesale by Redington.

Green died at the age of 70. He is said to have grieved over the death of his wife whom he did not long survive.

The concluding years of his business were apparently passed in a side street near Regent's Park. "It may perhaps have been a sort of semi-retirement," says Theo Arthur, "for the house which the remains of the firm occupied boasted of a little front garden and wooden palisading and in the parlour window a stage in all its glory of set scene was displayed."

From all the evidence which we now have available—or perhaps from the lack of it—the toy theatre seems to have come into existence fully developed. There do not appear to have been tentative efforts, experimental stages, continuous links of development. The first sight you have of it is the complete thing.

But obviously there must have been an experimental, tentative stage. On what

ONE OF GREEN'S SCENES WHICH SERVED FOR A MULTITUDE OF PLAYS
Dated June 1, 1837.

bright day did some happy genius think of peopling the toy stage with tiny cardboard characters for the delight and entertainment of young and old folk?

It is evident that the young folk amused themselves with toy stages before the days of the Juvenile Drama. They were home-made affairs and the actors were dolls and puppets. In the Victoria and Albert Museum, South Kensington, can be seen an excellent specimen, the gift of Lord Howard de Walden. The inscription states that it was in use at a ladies' school about the year 1800. It reproduces the old form of proscenium and the apron stage and is complete with scenery, 'cut-outs,' drops and wings elegantly done in pencil and water-colour in which one can trace the handiwork of the fair owners. The characters are small dressed dolls whose movements were controlled by wires. It is a much more primitive affair than anything of the penny plain school.

I am inclined to believe that the origin of the toy theatre with its cardboard characters must have been in Germany. Long before it made its appearance in England paper models had become popular playthings there, and there is a close resemblance between some of these models and the earliest kind of scenes and characters sold many years later in England.

"Some years before the close of the eighteenth century, German engravers and especially those of Augsburg," writes Karl Gröber in *Children's Toys of Bygone Days*,

> brought out a series of pictures meant only for cutting-out with which children could piece together all objects which came within the range of knowledge. Little figures were neatly cut out and suitably grouped and the background was then painted in. . . . The painting was left to the buyer to do. Then there were street scenes, hunting scenes, and sledging parties and children at play in the garden.

The specimens of these sheets exhibited in the Gewerbe Museum, Stüttgart, with their little groups of characters certainly bear a striking likeness to the English penny plain, twopence coloured sheets and one may reasonably suppose that some of these German sheets found their way to England and into the hands of the publishers of popular prints.

Some of the German model sheets were used for display in peep-shows. "The first model," says Karl Gröber,

> was "The Christmas Crib." Soon, however, purely secular subjects were chosen. The construction of such a peep-show was simple enough. The picture was cut out in its several planes. Each of these was then formed into a set piece and these sets were ranged one behind the other in proper perspective inside a wooden box which could be lighted from above. The background being very often broken into openings would be closed by pasting over them gaily-coloured mica and paper saturated in oil so that the lights placed behind would give the prettiest coloured effects. . . . They (the peep-shows) were brought to astonishing perfection in the eighteenth century and the range of subjects was enormous.

Late in the eighteenth century, according to Gröber, "one could get models of the theatre with figures for the newest plays for cutting-out purposes." It seems pretty clear, then, that the model of the toy theatre was popular in Germany long before it was known in England. I have seen pictures of little toy-theatre models produced in Vienna toward the close of the eighteenth century, with their stage boxes filled with fashionable and distinguished onlookers and their little stages crowded with cut-out characters. In many respects and allowing for the differences of theatrical architecture they resemble the English models of a much later date.

Another possible though less likely germ of the toy theatre is to be found in certain book illustrations later in the eighteenth century. In *The European Magazine* for 1786, for instance, there are some excellent engravings depicting scenes from current theatrical pieces. It is not difficult to imagine how these pictures with their striking and picturesque tableaux may have suggested themselves as being adaptable for cutting-out. The separation of characters from their background and the formation of miniature groups would naturally occur to the quick mind and then it would be only a short step to devise a stage and proscenium to enclose them.

This brings me to another point about the origin of the miniature stage.

I have often been assailed indignantly by enthusiasts for referring to the penny plain, twopence coloured drama as the "toy theatre." "The toy theatre!" they exclaim with scorn. "It was nothing of the sort; it was the miniature theatre." But they ignore the fact that the term "Juvenile Drama" was generally adopted by the publishers. Still, they may be right as far as the origin goes: the little theatre may have come into existence at first not for the amusement of the children but to satisfy the interest of their elders who were keen lovers of the stage and had little or nothing in the illustrated Press to make reproductions of their favourite plays and players a graphic reality to them.

It is the theory of those who regard the miniature stage as something more dignified than a toy for children that the grown-ups of a century or more ago gravely amused themselves by staging these little plays and manipulating the characters.

They are probably right in this matter of original purpose. It is to be remembered that in its early stage the toy theatre—the critics must forgive the use of the term—was not an inexpensive hobby, that children in those far-off days went to bed earlier in the evening, that they rarely went to the theatre except to see the pantomime, and that the first publishers like West, Hodgson, and Jameson took particular care not only to render the little characters life-like and spirited in their drawing but to secure a perfect likeness to the actors and actresses who created the parts. Such meticulous care would not have been necessary in the preparation of a mere toy for children.

It must be noted too that in the early sheets the names of the actors would appear.

CHARACTERS IN MRS HIBBERD'S "JULIUS CAESAR"
From the British Museum Collection

Each character would be described as "Mr So-and-So as So-and-So" (mentioning the name of the role) and the likenesses in many instances are as clear and unmistakeable as photographs. I have seen Liston's and Kean's and Munden's and T. P. Cooke's features reproduced with wonderful fidelity.

That the little stage did subsequently become a device wholly and solely for children I do not think can be disputed. It will be seen that after some years the publishers no longer took much care to reproduce the likenesses to stage favourites, although they still faithfully copied, apparently, the mounting and dressing of the productions in which they appeared. We may take it then, whoever was the inventor the idea soon gained enormous popularity. Many printers and publishers of valentines—once upon a time a very flourishing business—and cartoons of the Gilray and Rowlandson order were quick to take up the idea, and they rapidly copied each other, some of them not hesitating to pirate whole plays from their rivals.

Incidentally we read that in 1812 David Cox the artist, who at that time was a scene-painter at the Birmingham theatre, made a toy stage for young Macready (later the famous tragedian) whose father owned the theatre.

William West—whose work is dealt with separately elsewhere—started in the business in 1811. By the following year there were many competitors in the field and the piracy that went on shows that commercial honesty was not one of the strongest virtues of our forefathers. Green's "The Secret Mine," published in 1812, was, as I have mentioned, boldly taken from West. There was Mrs Hibberd who in 1811 even had published at least three plays: "The Forty Thieves" ("as played at the new theatre, Tottenham Street"), "Aladdin," and "Fairy of the Oak." There was H. J. Jameson who carried on business from 1811—30, publishing in all thirty-four plays, not many specimens of which are now in existence. He put out many plays between 1811 and 1815.

Burtenshaw who published for Green, in 1812 produced "The Golden Fish," a Covent Garden pantomime. Lloyd and Park were early publishers, so too was Spencer, who turned out some crude stuff. Later came Hodgson, one of the best of the publishers, then Skelt of immortal fame, Webb, Redington, Dyer, and others.

At the height of the popularity of the Juvenile Drama (about 1830) there were no fewer than fifty publishers engaged in the business. I have been able to trace a good many of these and in order to simplify matters and to provide a possible guide to collectors I have set them out alphabetically with the approximate dates (where known) in which they began business.[1] Some no doubt merely acted as publishers of other people's productions. With the more important of the publishers I have dealt separately elsewhere.

[1] See Appendix A

The list which appears at the end of the book will show at a glance what importance the Juvenile Drama business once assumed, for many of the firms were engaged exclusively in the trade. It is a notable fact that the business was entirely confined to London; I have found no record of any provincial publisher of such sheets.

Its decay and disappearance is a sad and curious affair. Skelt has been blamed for bringing it to ruin by cheapening the quality of the production and lowering the prices of the sheets; but though he did sell sheets at the price of one halfpenny it is not fair to ascribe all the blame to him, for Green, who began to publish a long time before Skelt, also published sheets at the same price, and although the majority of West's plain sheets were sold for a penny he also sold halfpenny sheets very early in the history of the business.

The fact is the Juvenile Drama could not resist the pressure of many diverse events and influences. Primarily the decline of the vogue is bound up with the advance of the English stage. Its vogue or entire history as a living thing and not as a subject of interest only to the collector or antiquary may be taken to extend roughly from the beginning of the century until (say) 1870.

Now in the history of the English theatre the greater part of this period is one of the most barren in the history of the drama and its close practically coincides with the turning point—the advent of new forces, new ideas, new conceptions and influences— the germ of what revolutionized and rejuvenated the art of playwriting and play production. It was the renaissance of the English drama—the coming of the Robertsonian "tea cup and saucer" comedy, followed by the appearance of Ibsen in this country and the influence which he exercised upon our native dramatists.

The drama had ceased to be a drama of violence and action, and of crude emotion; it was becoming the drama of ideas and of plain realism.

Here to my mind you have one of the most damaging of the many blows dealt at the Juvenile Drama; it was being deprived of the very substance upon which it had thrived—of the very drama which it had since its existence reflected.

Turn to the old lists and catalogues; the very titles of the plays indicate the paltry, gory, highly-coloured kind of drama upon which the toy theatre thrived in its heyday —" Black-eyed Susan," "The Blood-red Knight," "The Forty Thieves," "The Battle of Waterloo," "The Battle of the Alma," "The Pilot," "Red Rover," "The Smuggler," "The Hunter of the Alps," "The Brigand's Son," "Paul Clifford," "Jack Sheppard," "Three-fingered Jack," and scores more of the like.

You had here every opportunity for the introduction of exciting combats, violent encounters, sanguinary duels, the display of guns, pistols, swords, and other deadly engines, and every form of violent action. You had also the gorgeous Oriental processions and spectacular effects and trick changes so popular in pantomime.

GREEN'S PIRATED COPY OF "THE SECRET MINE"
Compare this with West's original.
From the British Museum Collection

ARTIST'S SKETCH AND THE FINISHED SHEET FOR WEST'S "THE SECRET MINE"
Dated May 6, 1812.
From the British Museum Collection

There were no discussions upon moral principles and abstract ideas or upon ethical or social questions. A good combat, duel, death, explosion, or other disaster took the place of philosophical discussions, literary dialogue and highbrow purpose.

The toy stage was obviously unsuited to subtle delineation of character. It was the place for simple, broad effects and the most primitive form of drama. Strong situation was much preferable to words, particularly as the dialogue had to be spoken by proxy and generally with one voice which could not indicate the change of speaker and character.

As some other writer has said:

> People ceased to care for the toy stage when it ceased to be representative of the real stage, when the drama developed along lines where its little rival could not hope to follow. On the other hand, for the display of dramatic situation, picturesque attitudes and scenic display the miniature theatre was unrivalled. The crude emotions of melodrama can be rendered if anything more effectively in action than in words.

In short, as William Archer pointed out, at this period of theatrical history "the picturesque melodrama of a mediæval, nautical, oriental order had given place to every-day drama with commonplace modern costumes not amenable to coloured treatment."

No longer were there picturesque robbers and brigands, gay soldiery, gorgeously caparisoned knights, magnificent Oriental potentates, highly-coloured peasantry, and dazzling highwaymen living, fighting, and carousing amid wild forests, frowning fortresses, extravagant castles, mountain torrents, haunted glens, and picturesque huts; instead you had plays filled with top hats, bowlers, and drab pantaloons and people talking in prosaic living rooms....

How could you colour these dull people and these drab scenes? Fancy a penny plain, twopence coloured version of one of Ibsen's social dramas! What would Pollock have made of Shaw's "Heartbreak House"? Where would be the chance for the verdant greens, the rich reds, the violent purples, the glorious blues of the paint box?

The miniature theatre has always been the topical reflection of the drama; it could not live perpetually upon its past successes. So this was the beginning of the end and other blows began to follow. The toy-theatre prints had been to the public what the pictorial Press is now, and prints were issued by hundreds of thousands. It is said that if there was a run on a particular play the printers would be kept working day and night to supply the sheets.

But now came the illustrated press, crude at first, but more satisfying perhaps as a mirror of the times than the theatrical sheets. Then came photography and a host of periodicals which found space for reproducing the figures and scenes from current theatrical productions.

By this time too, the quality of the prints, owing to intensive competition about which I shall have further occasion to speak, had sadly deteriorated and the reproduction was crude. The rise in the art of engraving and reproduction and the introduction of chromo-lithography killed the taste for the old sheets. The coloured pictorial poster was immensely more effective and powerful in its appeal to the popular imagination.

And the rapid growth of the cheap Press was another factor which militated against its prestige among young folk. Boys' journals began to appear giving new occupation for the winter evenings. The standard of education (now compulsory) too was rising and children engaged in home lessons had little time to devote to the colouring and preparation of their favourite plays.

And those who were young in those days assert that children began to be more active, restless and inquiring. The sedate old pastime by the fireside began to be too slow for them.

In its last stages the toy theatre declined into the issue of " penny packets " which I have described elsewhere—wretchedly poor and crude stuff without the slightest merit or artistic attraction.

The toy theatre, even had it been flourishing twenty years ago, could not have survived as a children's pastime in these days—the cinema would have killed it stone dead. What child would have tolerated its inaction in preference to the excitements and rapid animation of the screen?

I have tried in vain to interest children of the present day in the toy stage but have found them nearly all uninterested and unresponsive. They smile tolerantly and perhaps even a little contemptuously when they are told how children of the past generations used to amuse themselves with such a ' slow ' occupation.

Poor, poor children of a highly improved, hustled, and scientific age! In return I smile a little pityingly upon you.

CHAPTER FOUR

MAKING THE PLAY

WHEN one considers how cheaply the penny plain, twopence coloured sheets were retailed to the public the pains taken to secure accuracy in the miniature scenes and characters were really astonishing. The whole process was more elaborate than most people would imagine. This is how it was done.

The play to be reproduced was chosen from one of the current successes at the leading theatres—and here the publishers acted with the keen appreciation of the topical that marks the skill of the art editor of the modern illustrated press. All the big 'hits' of the theatrical season, all the favourite pantomimes, were to be obtained soon after their success had been established.

The book of the play was first condensed from the original script or, as seems probable in some instances, written from memory after a visit to the play. No doubt, as reading will show, this task was sometimes the work of the unskilled or of the hack, but frequently the author himself would boil down his own play for the use of the miniature stage. Can one imagine Noel Coward or Somerset Maugham performing a similar job in these days?

Some of these condensed versions were more briefly and sketchily prepared than others. Webb's books were of the shortest kind and so were Pollock's. One of Hodgson's book of words—"Chevy Chase," which is now very scarce—contained directions for colouring the costumes of the characters, which was information no other publisher thought of giving.

"The books of words supplied by these firms," writes Theo Arthur,

> were in their way masterpieces of adaptive art. How remarkably well-pruned for the youthful reader the speeches were!—all the big, big D's carefully suppressed.
>
> The daring of the theatrical stationers really knew no bounds. West even supplied a book of words for his edition of 'Tom and Jerry' to which Mr Bowdler could not have taken exception if it had been placed in his hands.

It should be noted that some of the best of the condensed versions were prepared by Webb himself.

The transpontine houses of the Surrey, the Royal Coburg (now the Old Vic), and Astley's furnished the majority of the subjects for the plays. The Olympic, over which

Mme Vestris reigned with such success, the Adelphi, the Lyceum—then quaintly known as the Royal English Opera House—and the New Theatre in Tottenham Street (where the Scala now stands) also contributed to the repertory.

It would astonish many believers in the 'palmy days' (says one writer) to see how many penny plain, twopence coloured melodramas figure on playbills which bore the illustrious name of John Kemble, Edmund Kean, Mrs Siddons, and Mrs O'Neill.

The book having been prepared, the artist would visit the theatre in order to make notes and sketches of the scenery and the costumes, and of the characters in their most striking attitudes. No doubt every encouragement was given by the managements, who must have benefited considerably by the free advertisement.

The greatest care appears to have been taken to ensure accuracy in the miniature productions. I have seen preliminary sketches for some of the early plays and they give every evidence of great pains taken by the artist.

It is certainly a fact, as I have said, that the actual likenesses were reproduced in the little cardboard characters. Those who have seen only the later reproductions of the toy theatre will find this difficult to believe, for no matter what the kind or quality of the later publishers, nor how the various artists differed in their styles, a strange family resemblance will be found among the characters. But in the work of the earlier publishers likenesses are to be distinguished which are astonishingly good, and the style of drawing was free and individual.

With the cheapening of the sheets and the consequent decline of quality less care appears to have been taken. "I do not think any of the juvenile prints can be relied upon as being the actual characters after 1840," says one authority.

After the draft sketches had been made a complete set of scenes, 'cut-outs,' wings, and characters was drawn. The process of reproduction in those days was slow and primitive, though when done by skilled artists and engravers it was capable of excellent results. The drawings had first to be transferred on to steel, copper, or zinc plates, first being backed with pigment and traced on to the prepared etching ground. The engraver then etched the lines with his needle, the plate was bitten with acid and after cleaning was ready for the proof print.

The sheets of characters became standardized into a uniform size after the first few years and were generally about eight and a half inches by six and a half, but the scenes were sold mostly in two sizes, one the same size as the sheets of characters, the other twelve inches by nine and a quarter.

Engraving the sheets was likewise a slow process, the plates having to be inked by hand. The ink was wiped off the surface with a rag, leaving ink in only the etched grooves. The impress was made with a roller. When the trade deteriorated and the plates became worn by much use the engravings were transferred to the lithographic

PROOF WITHOUT LETTERING OF WEST'S CHARACTERS IN "THE RUFFIAN BOY"
Showing West's colouring directions to the artist.
From the British Museum Collection

stone, which produced work far coarser in detail. It should be mentioned that the lettering on the sheets was generally the work of a special artist.

A few printers used wood-cuts; the results were very clumsy and inferior and none of the leading publishers (except Brett who largely helped to bring the trade into ruin) used the process.

The small sheets were at first sold mostly at a penny plain and twopence for the coloured. The large scenes coloured sold for threepence and were indeed cheap at the price, for very often the work was done with exceeding care and taste.

The " penny plain, twopence coloured " label therefore cannot be rightly applied to the whole of the toy theatre output especially as Green and Skelt brought down the price of the plain sheets to one halfpenny and for some time standardized the price among the trade.

So for a modest penny or two the purchaser became the possessor of a real coloured etching. One may easily guess that the low prices allowed for the smallest remuneration for those who had to colour the prints. Considering the price at which the sheets were sold the fee could not have been more than a halfpenny for the twopenny sheets and a penny for the threepenny. This was of course for hand work, when the sheet was completed by one person, and a more monotonous and tedious job even for one with the smallest amount of artistic skill and temperament could scarcely be devised.

Only four colours were used—gamboge, prussian blue, carmine, and black—but from these combinations could be made brown, a rich purple, and a wonderous green—" a green of such savoury greenness that to-day my heart regrets it," as Stevenson says of his own colouring efforts.

Many of the printers used to mix their colours with sugar, thus producing that rich, oily sheen to be noticed on some of the sheets. Some indeed made a great mystery of this colouring business, affecting to possess some magic secret in the preparation of the pigments. Much of this may be discounted, but I do not think amateur efforts ever equalled the rich, bold colouring of the professional artist, and it is possible there was a trade secret and much of the effect was no doubt due to the bold contrasts in colouring employed. The durability of the colouring is to be noticed. The hues of the old prints are as brilliant to-day as they were when they were first laid on over a hundred years ago. I am told that the pigments used for the paints cost twenty and thirty times as much to purchase to-day.

The colouring process when the business grew was carried out on Ford-like lines. The people employed in the work sat at a long table, each applying one colour only, and they were guided by the coloured proof supplied by the artist of the original until they were able to perform the operation mechanically. Whole families or groups of apprentices (we read) would assemble and the prints passed from hand to hand, each adding his or her own colour to the print. Rough masses of colour were put on by the less skilled, the final work and the flesh tinting falling to the more expert colourist.

Later in the century colour guides and stencils came into use for the work, considerably speeding up the output, but naturally the mechanical device deteriorated the quality of the production.

While no doubt a great deal of the original drawing in the later output of the Juvenile Drama was the work of inferior artists and of some indeed who could hardly claim to have any artistic ability at all, those pictures used by such pioneers as West, Jameson, and Hodgson were the work of artists of acknowledged eminence.

It will no doubt astonish many that these artists included George Cruikshank (born 1792 died 1878), his brother Robert (Isaac) Cruikshank (1789–1856), the brothers Heath, Flaxman, the artist and sculptor (1775–1826) who must during the time he was so employed have been a professor of sculpture at the newly formed Royal Academy, Charles Alfred Stothard (1786–1821) whose historical pictures were noted for their strict accuracy of detail, Robert Dighton (1752–1814) the portrait painter, caricaturist and etcher, William Finden (1787–1852), the eminent engraver who did a quantity of excellent book illustration and—most surprising of all—William Blake, mystic, poet, and artist (1757–1827).

Indeed, according to Godfrey Turner, writing in *The Theatre* in 1886,

> Blake was one of West's most industrious limners. The monogram combining the two letters 'W.B.' appears again and again on those penny sheets that were twopence when coloured. But the mannerism of Blake is almost sufficient—for remember it was a signature in spite of itself and was not likely to be obtruded. West's purpose was to subdue all these designs to one style, an ideal of his own.

The Heaths were actively engaged in drawing for Hodgson between 1820 and 1830. It was William Heath, famous in his day as a water-colour painter and etcher, who mostly did the colouring for West but Mr. Turner says he etched many of the figures also. Henry Heath excelled particularly in the drawing of horses and his 'combats' were very spirited and lively affairs. His military pictures are still well remembered. In "The Wild Boy," published by West, the free, flowing lines of George Cruikshank can easily be traced. "Tom and Jerry" was etched by Robert Cruikshank, who partially illustrated the original book.

It is strange that such a work as the *Dictionary of National Biography* mentions nothing of this form of artistic activity on the part of any of these artists, particularly as it occupied most of them during their prime, but the fact that they did this sort of work is well attested.

West is said to have paid his artists all round the sum of £2 for each plate of original drawings approved. This was the price received by Blake, Flaxman, and the rest.

WILLIAM BLAKE'S ORIGINAL DRAWING FOR WEST'S "THE BROKEN SWORD"
From the British Museum Collection

FINISHED SHEET FOR "THE BROKEN SWORD"
Note Blake's initials in lower right-hand corner. Dated November 4, 1816.
From the British Museum Collection

Among Blake's work in the collection noted by Ralph Thomas, is a set entitled " The principal characters in the new tragedy of 'Bertram,' in three plates." These pictures are very well drawn and engraved.

West also published "The principal characters in the grand melodrama ' The Broken Sword' as performed at the Theatre Royal, Covent Garden," published November 4, 1816. They were signed "W. B. *fecit*" and are beautifully executed.

The characters in "Guy Mannering" are also in Blake's style. They are variously dated from 1816–25. Scott's novel came out in 1815 and was dramatized in the following year.

Another sheet bearing the inscription "West's new theatrical characters sold—Magic—West *del*. W.B. *fecit*" is probably by Blake, for West's signature, as I have pointed out elsewhere, is nothing more apparently than a little harmless vanity.

Mr Thomas asserts that the brothers Cruikshank drew more for the Jameson firm than for West. "In fact," he says, "I believe all Jameson's are by the Cruikshanks."

Notes and Queries of October 1920 contains an interesting list of all the West prints which (according to Mr Thomas) are the work of the Cruikshanks. To this list are added some extensive and interesting notes. Mr. Thomas disputed Captain R. H. Douglas's claim that many of the Hodgson prints were by Cruikshank, remarking, " Such absurd attribution shows that the captain was no artist but was a mere collector with little knowledge of art or power of judging for himself."

"Incidentally," he adds, "I may mention that I have during the last few years completed the compilation of catalogues of every print I have seen of the juvenile theatrical series published by W. West which forms a MS quarto of about 200 pages."

Among the George Cruikshank drawings identified in *The Works of George Cruikshank Classified and Arranged with Reference to Reid's Catalogue,* by Capt. Douglas (Davy, 1903)—the work referred to by Thomas—are these:

Harlequin Brilliant and the Clown's Capers	(West)	1815
Harlequin and Fancy	,,	1816
Telemachus	,,	1825
Little Hunchback	,,	1825
Harlequin Whittington	,,	1828
Falls of the Clyde	(Jameson)	1818
Rob Roy	,,	1819
Undine	,,	1821
Don Juan	,,	1821
The Exile	,,	1822
Charles the Second	,,	1824
Invasion of Russia	,,	1825
Flying Dutchman	,,	1827
Two Gentlemen of Verona	(Hodgson)	1827

That some confusion exists as to the George Cruikshank contribution to the Juvenile Drama, particularly in regard to Hodgson's prints, is due to the fact that there was another artist with the same initials—George Childs.

Mr Thomas asserts that among a large number of prints attributed to the Cruikshanks and sold in Capt. Douglas's collection was a fine series issued by Hodgson, but they were in fact (he says) the work of Childs and were suspect because of their style.

Childs was an artist and scene-painter and there is little doubt that the scenes he drew for the miniature stage were the replicas of those which he invented for stage representation.

In *Notes and Queries*, 1916, by the way, Mr Thomas records the following reminiscence of Cruikshank:

> Many years ago I dined at the house of the scholar, author, and true lover of art, H. S. Ashbee. I sat between Mr and Mrs George Cruikshank.... The only bit of information I could get from him was that West's price to any artist for a quarto plate of characters was £1—no more. This price did not conform to Cruikshank's idea, he told me, which accounts for his having done so few for West.

It will be observed that this standard fee paid by West was only half that recorded by Godfrey Turner.

West himself spoke of George Cruikshank's work as casual and infrequent but, says Mr Turner, receipts with his signature which were sold as autographs even in Cruikshank's lifetime show that his work for West was regular and continuous over a period of at least two years.

It is recorded that on one occasion—and it is not known how often the incident was repeated—Cruikshank etched in his rapid and vigorous manner two plates or sheets of characters in one day.

It is suggested that Leech, the *Punch* artist, drew for the toy theatre, but I can find no evidence in support of this. Certainly no plates that I have seen bear any likeness to his well-known style.

As for the other artists of the Juvenile Drama such as those who supplied Green, Skelt, and Dyer, their names are buried for ever in anonymity.

DOUBLE SHEET OF WEST'S MINIATURE CHARACTERS
The characters were about 1¾ ins. high. Dated May 8, 1824.

From the British Museum Collection

ANOTHER OF WILLIAM BLAKE'S SHEETS
Dated June 15, 1824
From the British Museum Collection

CHAPTER FIVE

HOMAGE TO WILLY WEST

POOR Willy West has long since been gathered to his fathers and his plates have long been broken up. A complete collection of his engravings would be an invaluable addition to our knowledge of the aspect of the stage towards the beginning of the century and more particularly of the pantomime in its palmy days."

So wrote John Oxenford who, in a delightful appreciation of West's work in *The Era* Almanac of 1871, said his best characters were executed in a style of art which nothing of these days could approach.

Indeed every collector and nearly every writer upon this subject renders homage to this master of the Juvenile Drama business—the greatest man in its history and, as one authority remarks, "the aristocrat among theatrical stationers."

Do you remember Thackeray's reference to West in *Vanity Fair?* In Chapter LVI, writing about Georgy Osborne and young Todd, he says:

> In the company of this gentleman they visited all the principal theatres of the metropolis—knew the names of all the actors, from Drury Lane to Sadler's Wells; and performed, indeed, many of the plays to the Todd family and their youthful friends, with West's famous characters, on their pasteboard theatre.

They were famous characters indeed, though perhaps now forgotten.

Although there is much evidence, alas! that West had the 'Bohemian' habits too common in his period and that he allowed this to interfere with his business, he must have taken a true artist's pride in his trade. He prided himself particularly upon the accuracy of costumes depicted in his publications. No draughtsman was too good for the work he produced; no pains were too great to ensure the perfection of what he sold. West's colouring has been described as "a marvel of effectiveness."

Here is an instance of his thoroughness: When West issued his first sheets of scenes and characters for "The Miller and his Men" it was a poor performance. Most publishers, however, would have been content to let it go at that. Not so West. Dissatisfied with the quality of it he issued a new and vastly more spirited set the following year. Evidently West thought it worth while to spend as much money again as he had paid for the first set. This time he secured the work of George Cruikshank.

West began by issuing sheets of inferior execution but he steadily improved them as the years went on. Some say that his first play was "Baghvan Ho!" a melodramatic spectacle from Astley's, and dated February 17, 1811. This is not represented in the British Museum collection. The only sheets there of that play published by him are dated March 5, 1812.

West was far ahead of his competitors in the artistic quality of his publications. He was far in advance of the many rivals who rapidly followed him and who in time sadly declined from the high standard which he had set. The fact that others lowered their quality apparently meant nothing to him.

There is, of course, great difficulty in identifying the artists responsible for the majority of his prints, but it is confirmed that among those whom he employed were, as I have mentioned, the two Cruikshanks, Flaxman, and Blake. He could not have done better.

"To see West in his full glory," wrote William Archer in *The Drama in Pasteboard* (*Art Journal*, 1887),

> we must turn to the sheets in which are depicted the nautical dramas of the period. Of these " Black-eyed Susan" is the immortal type. Two other nautical dramas which West did with immense gusto are "The Pilot" and "Red Rover," adaptations of Fenimore Cooper's novels produced at the Adelphi towards the close of the 1820's.
>
> It seems that West went to nature for his studies for the likenesses of the performers are often recognizable unmistakably. Even in the character sheets as distinguished from the portrait plates (*i.e.*, those intended for tinselling purposes) the likenesses are often very spirited. . . . In West's characters we see the actors as they appeared to the admiring spectator.

Ralph Thomas remarks that West published scenes and characters of every play and pantomime of the time that captured any degree of popularity, and says that for execution and accuracy of drawing and general get-up he carried off the palm over all others.

Grimaldi figures constantly in the pantomimes. So do all the celebrated actors of the time such as Kean, Yates, O. Smith, the Keeleys, Blanchard, T. P. Cooke, Young, Kemble, Miss Ellen Tree, Wallack, Miss Kelly, Liston, and Munden. Kean was a great favourite of West. There were portraits of him as Macbeth, Othello, and Richard the Third.

Mme Vestris, the idol of the public, also figures in the collection. When her portraits were published she was in the height of her fame at the Olympic.

Some of West's pictures were really beautifully drawn, notably "The Abbot, or Mary Queen of Scots" (1820) "as performed at the Theatre of Varieties, Tottenham Street." They had great beauty and delicacy of line, are anatomically correct, and look charming when made up.

SCENE, WITH WING ATTACHED, FROM WEST'S "CORIOLANUS"
A fine example of architectural drawing and perspective. Dated December 14, 1824.

From the British Museum Collection

The scenes in "The Forty Thieves," "Blue Beard," "The Elephant of Siam," "Ivanhoe," "Korastikan," "Hyder Ali," are extraordinarily pretty and effective in their Oriental pageantry and floridity of design. The scenery is unrivalled in its touch and picturesqueness. The architectural drawing and perspective in the scenes of "Coriolanus," for instance, are singularly fine.

In "Casco Bay" the characters and scenes are very good. For one or two scenes there was such a demand that they are very scarce in these days.

"The publications of West," remarks Theo Arthur, "had one drawback—his figures were so large that they were out of place on the boards of the ordinary juvenile stage of commerce. West required a sort of patent theatre to himself."

Whether West himself drew any of the sheets which he published is a question which has often been discussed. The only evidence that he did is that some of his prints are marked "Wm. West *fecit*," or even "W. West *del. et sculpt.*" Many authorities, among them E. L. Blanchard and Godfrey Turner, assert that West did not draw at all, and I think they are right.

West's signature is probably a piece of harmless vanity or perhaps just a trick of the trade, or it is used for copyright protective purposes. He suffered a great deal from the piracy of rivals. There is no evidence that West could draw though he may have made rough sketches for his artist's use at the theatre. Besides, one finds his name signed to all varieties of style.

There is no doubt, however, that he took a very active part in the preparation of the original drawings. In the British Museum collection there are many original sketches as well as finished plates of West's plays in different stages of execution and colouring. Several of the uncoloured plates are scored with directions to the colourist and one (the drawing of T. P. Cooke as Orson) exists in what may be called its first coloured state with the instruction—perhaps in West's own hand—"colours a great deal brighter."

West's origin and preparation for the theatrical print business is obscure. According to one authority he was at one time a 'super' at the Olympic Theatre, though it is probable that his interest in stage matters led him thus to double his occupation.

He appears to have begun business at Exeter House, 13 Exeter Street, Strand and to have run a circulating library there. It was in the heart of the then Theatre-land. Thence he removed to the "theatrical print warehouse" at 57 Wych Street, opposite the Olympic Theatre, whose productions he reproduced in miniature. The great theatres of Drury Lane, Covent Garden, and the Lyceum were not far off. Bush House now covers what is practically the site of this cradle of the Juvenile Drama.

West's catalogue makes quaint and interesting reading. It is entitled "West's Catalogue of Original, Tragic, Fancy, and Comic Characters as performed at the Theatres

Royal Covent Garden, Drury Lane, Lyceum, Surry (*sic*), Astley's, Sadler's Wells, etc., etc."

In the catalogue he advertises "New Plates of pantomime tricks, ditto miniature equestrian combats, plates of theatrical robbers, ditto small theatrical combats, ground pieces, horizons, plates of small sea-waters and boats, ditto fairy cars, ditto magic characters, new plates of good and evil geniuses, and all theatrical representations that will be reproduced."

The catalogue adds:

"The whole of the characters are Finely Engraved from Original Drawings in their Exact Costumes and Printed on Fine Drawing Paper purposely for Colouring and Published by Permission of the Proprietors of the Different Theatres."

For several years West must have carried on business at both addresses. Some of his sheets issued from Wych Street are dated as early as 1812 and some dated from Exeter Street are as late as 1822.

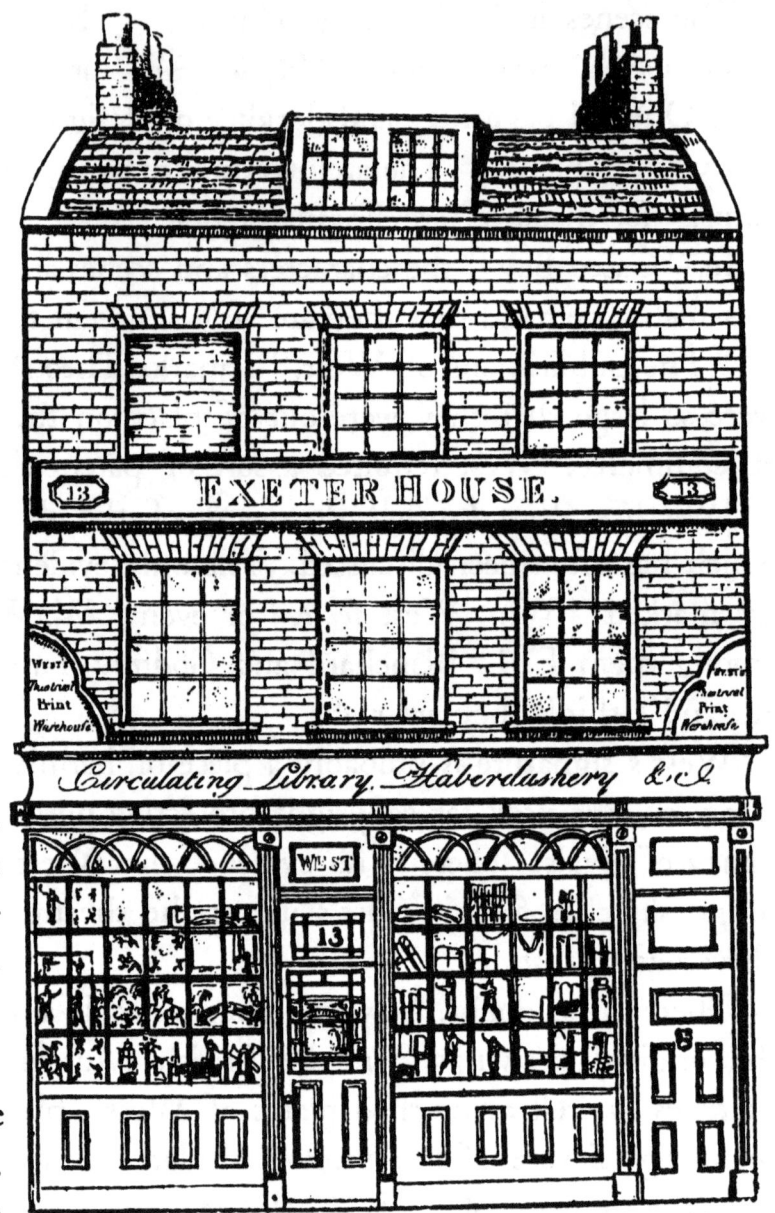

WEST'S SHOP IN EXETER STREET, REPRODUCED AS A PANTOMIME 'TRICK' SCENE
Dated October 21, 1813.

It is clear that West was an erratic man of business and that if his trade was subject to violent fluctuations it was probably largely his own fault. Ralph Thomas suggests that he got into some sort of trouble in 1824 (? 1830) as he published no *new* plays that year but re-dated many old ones instead.

There is another example of West's queer way of doing business. Mr Thomas in *Notes and Queries* in 1916 recalls a conversation that he had with George Cruikshank when the latter was an old man.

To Mr Thomas's remark, "West seems to have been a dilatory sort of man," Cruikshank replied, "Yes, he was. The boys used to go into his shop and abuse him 'like anything' for his frequent delays in publishing continuations of his plates."

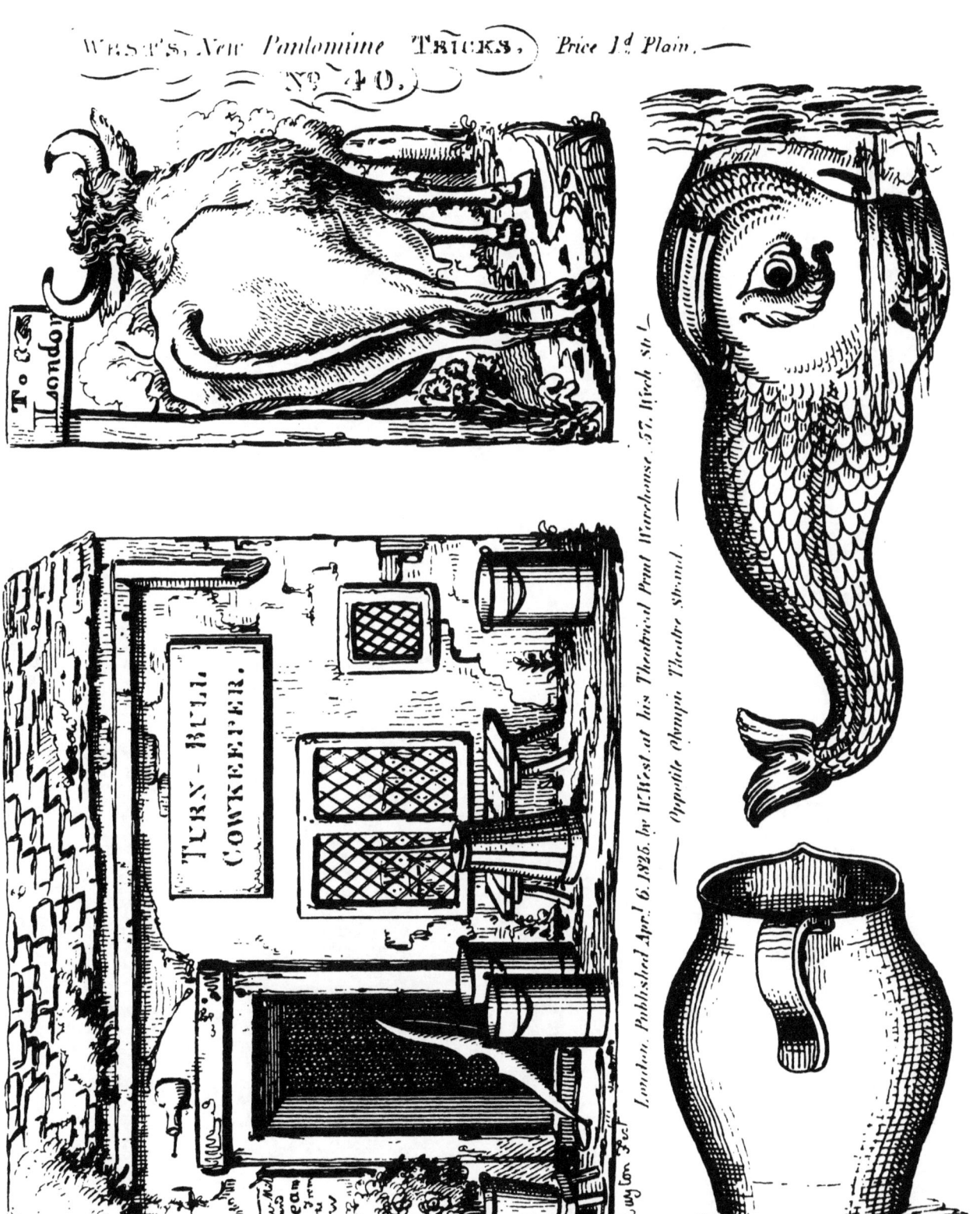

WEST'S "NEW PANTOMIME TRICKS"
An excellent example of T. Layton's work. Dated April 6, 1825.

A SHEET OF WEST'S PANTOMIME 'TRICKS' DATED JULY 14, 1827

"No wonder the boys complained when we know some of the facts," comments Mr Thomas. "West's characters and scenes in 'The Pilot' were published in 1828 but the side scenes were not issued until 1833. 'The Forty Thieves' he issued in 1819 but plate 6 is dated and did not appear until 1827."

In the circumstances it is no wonder that the business ultimately fell into decay.

In all, West issued one hundred and seven plays costing one penny, twopence, and threepence a sheet. A few sheets were even sold at one halfpenny. All his sheets are dated and range in size from 6¾ inches by 8¼ to nearly double that size.

I have compiled a list of the plays as far as I have been able to trace them.[1] Only one or two of them are missing. The list is interesting as a record of the output of the foremost of all theatrical publishers and as a record, besides, of the most important theatrical productions on the London stage over a period of about twenty years.

A great deal of mystery surrounds the life of West. About his marriage, for instance. It is stated that his wife was a well-known actress, but this is probably a mistake. William Archer says that the "famous Mrs West" who figured in the collections in the character of Berengaria was the wife of an actor. There is mystery too as to West's end. I cannot trace the date of his death nor, indeed, exactly what became of him in

[1] See Appendix B

his later years. Living authorities have been unable to glean very definite information.

One writer—I think it is Stanley Nott, writing in *The Drama* (New York)—mentions that 'Mr and Mrs West' in their later days were seen walking the streets of London in a state of wretchedness.

An authority with whom I have discussed the matter—Mr E. P. Prior—throws doubt on this story. Mr Prior says that in his old age West was afflicted with consumption and was unable to carry on the business himself in Wych Street.

A pathetic picture of West in his last days is drawn by Edward Draper in his *Scenes and Characters* (1868). He says:

> A short time before his death he (West) commenced selling off his stock at ridiculously low prices. The poor old man could be heard gasping for breath behind a small screen which divided his death-bed from the public portion of his shop. There might thus be had, capitally drawn and, when coloured, as gorgeous as summer flowers, engraved character portraits of all the dramatic celebrities of the past generation and these—we allude to the larger prints—were really good characteristic portraits; not as now, mere outrageous, idealised figures sprawled into impossible attitudes to fill four corners of the sheet.

The writer mentions that shortly before West's death Albert Smith, the once popular novelist and lecturer who made many references to the Juvenile Drama in his books. happening to pass along Wych Street entered the shop and purchased a copy of every print that remained on sale.

After West's death the shop appears to have been for some time carried on by Mrs Stokes, who had been his housekeeper. A strong, hefty woman she was able to carry on the somewhat trying business alone while West was lying ill on the premises.

Some play sheets bear her name and are marked "Stokes, late West." Among them are "The Pilot" and "Olympic Revels," both dated 1832, and as the list shows, they were the last plays issued by West himself. Mrs Stokes's business must have existed on West's stock entirely.

Many of West's plays were subsequently taken over by the industrious Skelt and altered. It is said that after the business was given up many thousands of sheets of plays and characters were disposed of to shopkeepers for wrapping purposes. It is enough to make the collector weep.

There is a legend that West in his will directed that his plates should be destroyed upon his death. It is frequently referred to by writers on the subject.

I have read that West presented, in the height of prosperity, a toy theatre perfectly fitted with a full stock of accessories to the children of the Royal Family. It would be interesting to know what became of this interesting specimen of Willy West's art and whether it is still in existence.

A STOKES SHEET

Characters in "Olympic Revels." Dated March 20, 1832.
From the British Museum Collection

CHAPTER SIX

HODGSON, THE IMMORTAL SKELT, AND SOME OTHERS

SOME of the best work of the toy theatre was turned out by Orlando Hodgson, who began business in 1822 and continued until 1832, when the business was taken over by Fairburn ultimately to get into the hands of the all-devouring Skelt. Hodgson was one of the most illustrious figures of the palmy days of the Juvenile Drama.

SCENE FROM HODGSON'S "CHEVY CHASE" DATED OCTOBER 20, 1832

Hodgson was in business at 10 Newgate Street and 43 Holywell Street, Strand, as a publisher of juvenile books and theatrical portraits. He issued in all twenty-five plays.

Many of Hodgson's pictures were of high artistic merit. His characters were, generally speaking, larger than the average. Some of his earlier plays were not very good; in "Montrose, or Children of the Mist" (July 10, 1822) the characters were crudely drawn, although the scene work was excellent. But there came an improvement in the quality of the productions and some of his big scenes (price 3d, plain) which measure about ten inches by twelve inches are really beautifully drawn and do great credit to the artist, George Childs, whose signatures "G.C.," as I have already observed, has often given rise to the belief that his pictures were drawn by George Cruikshank. The use of large, bare, white spaces made them most suitable for colouring, and when so treated by a skilled colourist many of them look quite charming.

The scenes drawn by T. Layton were very fine specimens of work.

Some of Hodgson's best figure work is exhibited in "Guy Fawkes" and "Ali Pacha," both published in 1822. The characters are drawn with freedom and spirit, and in many cases with a delicacy of line that lends itself admirably to colouring, which was tastefully done by Hodgson's men.

A year later in some of the plates of "Romeo and Juliet" there is a distinct falling off in style and quality although one or two of the more grotesque characters exhibit a pleasing spirit of caricature. The "Ali Pacha" Oriental characters are delightful examples of bold and free drawing. Some of the pantomime tricks published in 1825 are beautifully designed.

One of Hodgson's most striking efforts was a tableau picturing the burning of Troy in "The Giant Horse." The great figure of a horse fills the background. From its back protrude somewhat stolidly the helmeted heads of soldiery. Cohorts of warriors are lined up in front and they are being spurred onward by a tragic-looking maiden who brandishes a torch, and a nobly whiskered warrior who points to the dreadful conflagration on the left. The sky has an ominous blackness which, though tragically impressive, is a hindrance to the work of colouring. On the whole this is a fine imaginative bit of drawing reflecting great credit upon its artist.

Many of the early plays were inscribed "Hodgson's theatrical characters from original drawings." The characters were mostly on the large side, some being about four inches high. Though most of the men were pleasing enough to look at, one regrettable feature was the exceeding plainness of the women, who were generally tall and angularly built and nearly all with long, narrow, and expressionless faces.

Some of the first work issued by Hodgson were long panoramic strips about fifteen inches by six, descriptive of exciting equestrian combats. They were well drawn with spirit and imagination, depicting prone bodies, warriors lying in fierce agonies, fearful looking gentlemen in armour engaged in mortal combat.

Whether these panoramas were intended for use on the miniature stage or merely for framing purposes I do not know. They may have been designed for use as an exciting climax to the play.

CHARACTERS IN HODGSON'S "ROMEO AND JULIET"
Dated May 16, 1823.

FINALE IN "ALADDIN"
Published by Orlando Hodgson January 19, 1832.

AN EXCELLENT EXAMPLE OF GEORGE CHILDS' WORK
A scene used in many of Hodgson's plays. Dated March 17, 1823.
From the British Museum Collection

ANOTHER EXAMPLE OF JAMESON'S EARLIER AND CRUDE WORK
Dated August 24, 1811.
From the British Museum Collection

CHARACTERS FROM HODGSON'S "GUY FAWKES" (1822)

SCENE FROM O. HODGSON'S "GIANT HORSE"
Double plate, price 2d.

JAMESON SHEET BEARING THE DIRECTION: "HAT NOT HALF SO LARGE"
Probably an artist's proof.
From the British Museum Collection

A GEORGE CHILDS' SCENE
Dated June 25, 1822.
From the British Museum Collection

HODGSON'S SCENE FROM "ALADDIN"
Drawn by George Childs.
From the British Museum Collection

A CRUDE EXAMPLE OF JAMESON'S WORK
Dated November 6, 1811.
From the British Museum Collection

Another contemporary of West and the publisher of some very creditable work was H. J. Jameson, who reigned from 1811 to 1830. He published altogether thirty-four plays of which very few specimens exist.

Some were crudely drawn. Jameson's "The Miller and his Men" (1815) was very poor compared with some other versions of the famous play. "The Americans" (May 1811), which was one of his first productions, was also a very crude piece of work, the drawing being thin and hesitant. There was an improvement in the later plays, notably in "Bertram" (1816). As I have noted elsewhere the work of nearly all Jameson's plays is believed to have been that of the two Cruikshanks. A marked characteristic of the George Cruikshank style is the beady-eyed expression of the characters. Jameson's other plays include "Comus" (1811), "The Illuminated Lake" (1812), "Charles the Bold" (1815), and "Don Juan" and "The Corsair" (1824).

Another of West's rivals was Mrs Hibberd, who had a circulating library at 2 Upper Carlton Street, Marylebone. Excepting Mrs Stokes, who carried on the West business in its last days, she was apparently the only woman engaged in the toy theatre trade, and the work for which she was responsible entitles her to more notice than she has so far received.

She issued plays from 1811 to 1814. One of her best productions in 1811 was "The Forty Thieves" ("as played at the New Theatre, Tottenham Street"). Her "Julius Caesar" was quite a creditable piece of work, the drawing of the characters being bold and excellent, and there is indeed a definitely individual style about her productions.

One of the notable earlier publishers was Park of 47 Leonard Street, Finsbury, yet he also is one of those of whom very little is really known. It is of particular interest to recall that he was the publisher to whom W. G. Webb was apprenticed. He carried on an extensive general printing, engraving and lithographic business.

Park as a journeyman drew for Cole of 10 Newgate Street who, in turn, had taken over some of Hodgson's business. Park's first drawings were rather crude; they improved later, for he was a fair engraver and although he employed other artists he always insisted on drawing the faces of the characters himself in dry point and the facial modelling is very good. One writer notes "a certain arabesqueness" about Park's sheets.

Park published a fair number of dramas and supplied most of the favourite plays of the Royal Coburg Theatre. He specialized mostly in plays of the vivid "blood and thunder" type. His "Raymond and Agnes, or the Bleeding Nun" and "The Wood Demon" were really capably done. "The Spectre Bride" had some fine ghost effects.

Park is said to have had a son in the business in St John's Road, Hoxton, but I have not been able to trace him or any of his work.

A contemporary of Hodgson and West was Dyer of 13 Dorset Crescent, Hoxton

New Town and 109 Aldersgate Street. He was active in the year 1828. Some of his cut-out scenes were notably good. His son, Dyer junr., carried on business at 33 (later 55) Bath Street, City Road.

Another publisher of some note but of relatively small output was R. Lloyd who conducted a "juvenile dramatic repository" at 40 Gibson Street, near the Royal Coburg Theatre. He was a brother of the Lloyd who founded *Lloyd's News* and in another branch of his activity published many 'bloods.'

We now come to the prolific and immortal Matthew Skelt—immortal, perhaps, because Stevenson chose to enshrine the name in his essay as a synonym for the Juvenile Drama and to coin the term 'Skeltery' as descriptive of its peculiar charm and characteristic qualities.

"The name of Skelt," he wrote, "has always seemed part and parcel of the charm of his productions. . . . Indeed this name appears so stagey and piratic that I will adopt it boldly to design these qualities."

And he goes on to talk about the scenery of Skeltdom:

> A botanist could tell it by its plants. Its hollyhock was all pervasive, running wild in deserts; the dock was common and the bending reed; and overshadowing all these were poplar, palm, potato tree, and *Quercus Skeltica*—brave growths. . . . It was in the occidental scenery that Skelt was really all himself. It had a strong flavour of England; it was a sort of indigestion of England and drop scenes and I am bound to say was charming.

How well and accurately that describes the essential qualities of Skelt's plays whatever their origin, and how it calls to mind at once his panorama of bosky forests, wild, entangled growths, brave battlements, and homely cottage interiors with their "rosaries of onions, the gun and powder horn, and corner cupboard"—the inseparable features in the scenes of his stirring dramas.

There really is something rather magnificent about Skelt. I subscribe neither to the doctrine that he was, artistically speaking, one of the great ones of the Juvenile Drama nor to the heresy that he was the villain of the piece—*i.e.*, that he reduced the business to ruin by bringing down the price of the prints—but I do assert that he has some vast, picturesque quality possessed by no other publisher of his kind.

There is to begin with his prolific output and his octopus habit—his enterprising method of taking over the businesses of others and adding them to his own.

During his career in this line he published no fewer than fifty-three plays, an output up to then exceeded only by his predecessor West. They were all done in copper-plate.

But not a great deal of Skelt's was original work. A great number of his plays were those of Hodgson altered. He also bought up among others the businesses of Lloyd (as will be seen in the plates of "Therese or The Orphan of Geneva") and Park

A LLOYD PLAY TAKEN OVER BY SKELT

M. AND M. SKELT'S SCENE FROM "TIMOUR THE TARTAR"

M. AND B. SKELT'S SCENE FROM "DER FREISCHUTZ"

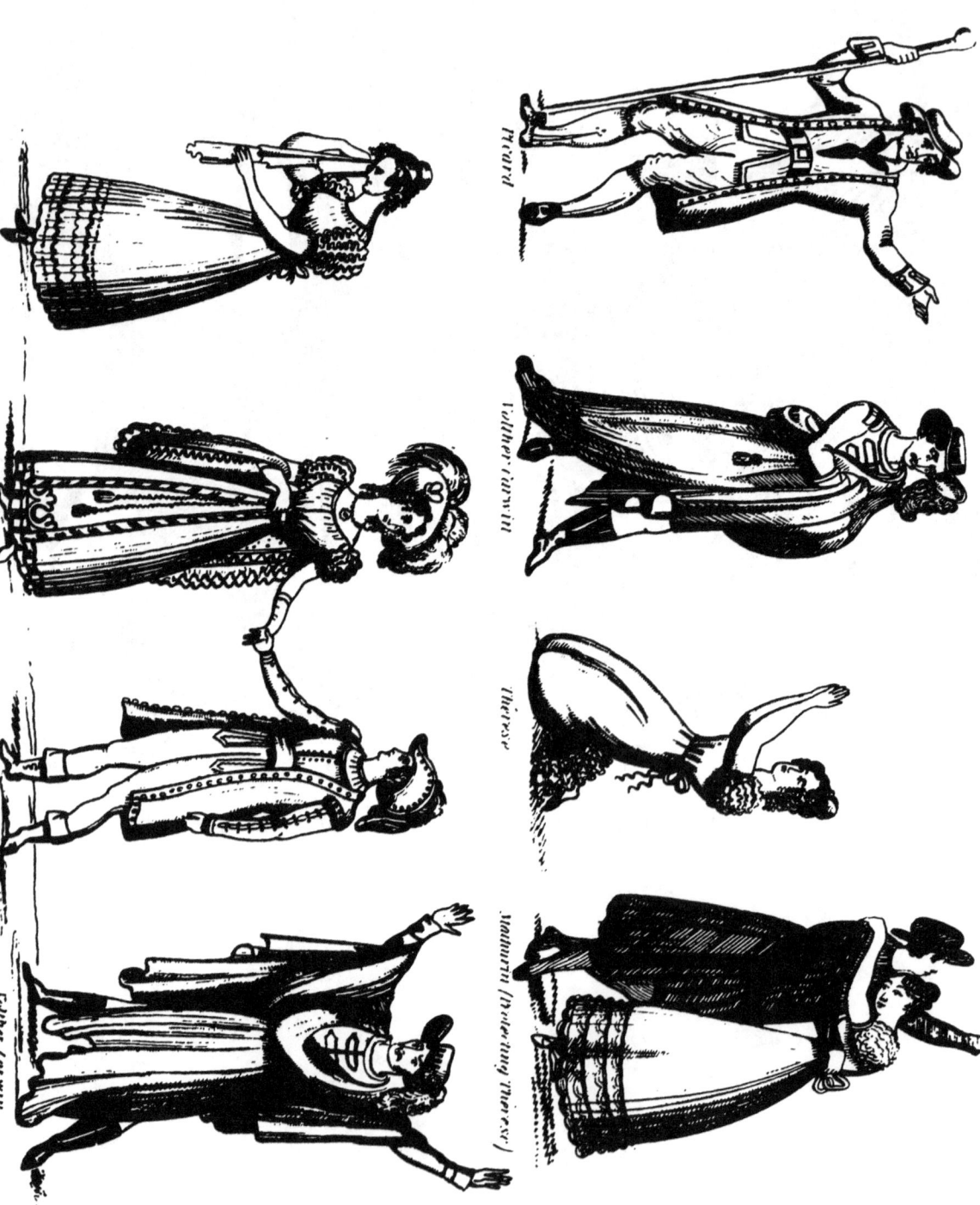

"THÉRÈSE, OR THE ORPHAN OF GENEVA"
A Lloyd's Play taken over by Skelt.

and he took over some of Dyer's plates. Indeed Skelt always seemed to be industriously on the look-out for some other business to acquire.

Skelt had the damnable habit of not dating his plays which makes it difficult to trace their chronological order.

It is odd that this man so closely identified with the Juvenile Drama business should have originated from a direction so remotely connected with it. He was originally a shoemaker and at his little shop in the Minories at 11 Swan Street he began to exhibit in his window the plays of Park and West as a side-line. Finding this a more paying business than cobbling, about 1840 he started publishing plays on his own account and he soon exhibited an activity that made him outstrip all his competitors.

He sold his plain sheets at the reduced prices of a halfpenny which, it has been said, brought about an intensive competition that ultimately resulted in the ruin of the business. This assertion, however, is hardly fair to Skelt; it would be truer to say that he popularised the sale of the prints.

Although Skelt's plays were the work of different artists who, from all I can gather were very poorly paid, a common quality seems to be exhibited in them. As Theo Arthur remarks (*The Era* Almanac, 1891) "Skelt went in strongly for pose appropriate to the occasion, favoured scragginess, and produced distinctly plain female characters." Stevenson also remarks upon the "extreme hard favour" of his heroines. These ringletted, high-waisted damsels have certainly a rather meagre and forbidding if not disagreeable look.

Some of Skelt's greatest successes were in those plays that had an Oriental flavour with many picturesque processions and spectacular displays. You saw him at his best in such pieces as "Blue Beard," "Aladdin," "Timour the Tartar," and "The Forty Thieves."

"An especial favourite," writes Theo Arthur, "was 'Der Freischutz,' a play founded upon the same legend which Weber set to music. So popular was the play that at one period it was to be seen at two of the principal theatres and there were burlesque versions of it playing elsewhere."

There was a particular drawback to this play—the quantity of coloured fires required while the magic bullets were being cast producing often not only an awe-inspiring effect but temporary asphyxia among the audience and the stage manager and his assistants.

The back scene of the Wolf's Glen in this play, if I may say so, exhibits the Skeltic temperament in the extreme. Look at those vast rock formations, the moss-grown ridges and curious lichens, the odd fir trees, the rigid waterfall, and the blasted oak upon which perches the most stolid-looking owl known to the fauna of Skeltdom.

But as an effect of the imagination I think the palm must be awarded to the last scene in "Mary, Maid of the Inn." Here are drama and action if you like! What terrible events this scene crowned I know not, but it must have been something desperate in the extreme. Within a yard or two of the shore a sailor clings to a rock. A foot or two away and in imminent danger of dashing itself to pieces against the lighthouse is a curious looking craft to the rigging of which clings a girl. Whether she is menacing or helping the sailor is not clear.

The seas are raging with a peculiar curly and solid kind of wave and the heavens send out dreadful lightnings. In the foreground are grouped in neat divisions to the left and the right men brandishing torches who might be either mariners or pirates or smugglers, while a well-clad and befeathered gentleman on the extreme right stands by with a complacent air of detachment and approval.

"Harlequin Little King Pippin," a pantomime which represented London of the period in a vast number of scenes, was also highly popular. Skelt's "Jonathan Bradford" was one of the most difficult problems ever put before the producer of the juvenile theatre, for in the sensational scene depicting the murder of Mr Hayes the tiny stage had to be divided into four compartments. Some of our modern producers are evidently not so modern as they imagine.

There was another way in which Skelt showed himself to be a man of energy and enterprise—he introduced many members of his family into the business.

His first plays bore the inscription "Published by M. Skelt." Later he took a relative into the business and the firm became known as M. and B. Skelt. Then Matthew Skelt went out of the business and the prints were published by B. Skelt who, Ralph Thomas presumed (in *Notes and Queries*, August 27, 1898) "burst up like the explosion in 'The Miller and his Men.'" "But," he adds, "there must have been some salvage from the general wreck for there were some plays published by E. Skelt without any address."

It is sad that this once flourishing business came to grief but it had persisted until the popularity of the toy theatre had begun to decline and it had, I am afraid, got into unskilled hands. Certain plays all drawn and engraved ready for publication were never issued.

I have seen a letter written by E. Skelt to the elder Webb, dated some time in 1867, in which the writer expressed the hope of reviving something of the trade, but apparently the project came to nothing and this, the last of the Skelts, died about 1890. At the time of his death he was a timekeeper at Waterlow's the printers.

I do not know when the remains of the Skelt business were sold up, but Webb had Skelt's plates of "Aladdin" and sold them with Skelt's name taken out and his own inserted. Webb acquired many other of Skelt's plays but never issued them. For some reason he destroyed certain of the plates. "I don't know why," says Mr H. J. Webb. "I only know that they were those I wanted him to keep."

SKELT'S LAST SCENE IN "MARY THE MAID OF THE INN"

CHARACTERS IN "LITTLE KING PIPPIN"

One peculiar distinction about the original Skelt was that he held the copyright of the popular play "Captain Ross," a Robinson Crusoe-like drama and no one could perform it without his permission. It is said that the majority of Skelt's original plays were the work of two brothers (name unknown) both of whom died in the workhouse.

Round about the time that Matthew Skelt was flourishing J. L. Marks was carrying on business at 17, Artillery Lane, Bishopsgate; 91, Long Lane, Smithfield; and 23, Russell Court, Drury Lane. Between 1839–45 he published theatrical portraits and he carried on business for some considerable time. It is said that he engraved his own plates; at least they were signed "Marks *fecit*" and some of them were very well done. His "Life in London" is very good.

Hereabouts we come to Redington, who was the predecessor and father-in-law of the still living Pollock, and his name therefore links us with the present.

Redington was originally a printer and he began about 1838 by selling Skelt's plays as a side-line at 208, Hoxton New Town, the same quaint little shop which is now known as 73 Hoxton Street. There he conducted a "wholesale and retail theatrical and print and tinsel warehouse."

It was because he found it difficult to obtain supplies from Skelt that he decided to start in business for himself. So he took over a quantity of Green's plays, altering the names on the plates. The bulk of the collection is by Green. Some of them are by Park. Sanderson of Berwick Street acted as Redington's wholesaler. Altogether Redington published seventy-three different plays at a halfpenny a sheet, eighteen at a penny a sheet and sixteen pantomimes. The plates of many of these are no longer in existence.

Mr Redington appears to have combined with his business a multitude of other occupations. He advertised himself as printer, bookbinder, stationer, tobacconist, circulating librarian, and fancy depository proprietor. He also dealt in "haberdashery of every description," and announced himself as ready to repair all kinds of jewellery. Here is one of his many flowery announcements taken from the back cover of one of his plays:

Large penny scenes as large as the twopenny of the following plays:
"Don Quixote," "Waterman," "Charles the Second," to be followed by others in rapid succession.
Drop scenes, top drops, orchestras, foot and water-pieces, ready-made tricks etc.
New ½d, 1d, 3d, and 4d stage fronts (the above 4d front builds higher than any published at 6d).
Single portraits, combats, fours, sixes, twelves, sixteens, fairies, horse soldiers, soldiers, portraits, clowns, rifles, &c.
The above plain and coloured. Stages and stage fronts built or flat, slides, firepans and lamps.
Blue, green, amber, and every coloured fires.

Redington's theatre provided a wide variety of choice. He specialised in short pieces like "Charles the Second," "The Waterman," and "The Lord Mayor's Fool"—

which I have seen described as "a singularly idiotic work"—which were presumably curtain-raisers to the longer plays and pantomimes of the period.

The artistic quality of Redington's plays was not perhaps very high in comparison with the work of such publishers as West and Hodgson, but I do not think his plays merit the description applied by one critic—"For uncompromising ugliness and squareness of form Redington 'took the cake,' the productions of Green running him very close on the score of being 'out of drawing.'"

Personally I like Redington's plays for the sake of their occasional quaint crudeness.

When Redington died in 1877 his business was taken over by Benjamin Pollock, who married his daughter. After Redington there is no considerable firm in the history of the Juvenile Drama.

Some years before Redington died there came a new form of competition in the field of the toy theatre. It was one of the influences that led to the ultimate decay of the business.

This was when Edwin J. Brett began publishing the popular weekly, *The Boys of England*, in 1866. He published a string of similar periodicals including *The Boys of the World* and *The Young Mechanic,* all of which had a great vogue and from which Brett made a handsome profit.

Then Brett conceived the idea of issuing plays for the toy stage in instalments. The first was "Alone in the Pirates' Lair," a production in wood-cut. The first instalment was given away with *The Boys of England,* November 27, 1866. The grand event was notified in the following announcement:

> Given away—To the boys of England a complete new play entitled "Alone in the Pirates' Lair" consisting of eight scenes, seven sheets of characters, six wings, foot pieces and a large stage front. N.B. The above entertaining gift is specially designed for young readers.

The play was given away in four instalments and subsequently it was produced in colour and sold complete in sets of sixteen characters and scenes for sixpence the set, and this was the beginning of Brett's collection to be sold at prices much lower than any other dealer had ever published.

Mr Brett also planned to sell toy stages on a grandiose scale and the following announcement must have gladdened the heart of many a boy with great expectation:

> The Stage! The Stage! We have great pleasure in informing our readers that we are now making arrangements to supply them with large stages suitable for the new play "Alone in the Pirates' Lair" also with large stage fronts designed and engraved expressly for our boys. We believe the usual prices would be about 2s each but we have determined to supply our readers with stage and stage fronts for only fifteen stamps (1s 3d). In the course of the week we shall open agencies throughout the United Kingdom. Our boys are requested not to send stamps until our arrangements are quite complete.

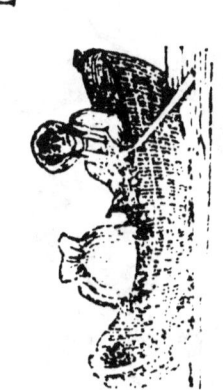

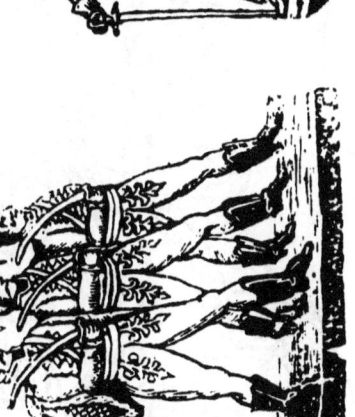

MILLER AND HIS MEN

IN TWO PLATES; PLATE 2nd.

Printed and Published by J. QUICK,
4, Dukes Court Paviors Alley Union Street,
Blaak Friars Road

Also sold at 41, Fashion Street, Spitalfields
and 18, Mill Street, Lambeth.

"NEARLY THE WORST OF ANY PUBLISHER"
Quick's woodcut version of "The Miller and his Men."

From the British Museum Collection

SHEET FROM "MAZEPPA" GIVEN AWAY WITH "THE BOYS OF ENGLAND"

In the next number of the paper it was announced:

> Our theatres are strongly constructed of wood by the largest stage manufacturers of London. Each theatre will consist of two sliding traps, place for lamp, roller for green curtain, grooves for back and side screen etc. Sawing and planing machines are employed to prepare the wood but as a short time must elapse before our immense order for 50,000 of the stages is completed our readers will be wise if they send at once to the bookseller as they will be supplied as each order is received.

But the plan of flooding the nurseries and playrooms of the country with these wonderful stages was still further delayed, for in a later number appeared the following notice which must have cruelly chilled boyish expectation:

> Our stages are not yet completed. They will be ready in a few days. We must therefore request our boys not to send any more stamps to our office for them but to order them from their newsagent and they will receive the stages when ready with their books.

Sad to say the stages apparently never were ready. A later announcement stated that there had been a hitch somewhere and all further reference to the great plan was dropped for a long time. However Mr Brett went on issuing plays. "Jack Cade" was the next produced. It was in seven large sheets of scenes and eight sheets of characters. They were crudely done and were much inferior to any sheets issued by any of the reputable publishers.

Further plays included "Tom Daring, or Far from Home," "King Arthur, or the Knights of the Round Table" (1870), "The Skeleton Horseman," "The Giant of the Blue Mountains," "Harlequin Jack and his Seven Brothers" (1872). In 1874 came the inevitable "The Miller and his Men"—an inferior production—and later "Robinson Crusoe," "The Forty Thieves," "Bluebeard," "Mazeppa," and "The Roadside Inn."

The prices of these completed plays was sixpence plain and one shilling coloured. They were sold coloured and cut out ready for use at 2s. 6d. and 3s. 9d. the set. No other dealer could possibly compete against such prices and from this time the trade began sensibly to decline. Brett did good work in supplying the boys of England with cheap, wholesome and entertaining literature, but in running this side-line for advertising purposes he dealt a heavy blow at the popularity of the toy theatre, for what boy would pay even a halfpenny a sheet for his plays when he could get them gratis with his favourite journal?

Others who carried on business in the days of the decline included Quick, whose work was nearly the worst of that of any publisher. He used wood cuts and his characters were small, amateurishly drawn and badly printed. Perkins was another publisher of wood cuts. Hawley issued some 'orchestras' and sheets of characters designed to move with the aid of pins and cotton, a device that apparently never caught on—or perhaps which never worked.

One of the last to enter the field was Matthews of Churchfield Road, Acton, who did not begin publishing until 1887. His plays, I believe, were all copies from the work of other publishers. He re-issued several of Park's sheets in lithography, and continued to publish plays as late as 1895.

This list may be closed with the names of Andrews and Co. and Clarke, the publishers of the penny packets which brought cheapness down to the lowest level. There were even plays published at a halfpenny complete with book of words, scenes, and characters, while in the Globe series there were complete plays for one penny. All that can be said of them is that they were cheap and nasty. They had nothing to commend them and have little interest for the collector. One or two obscure and piratical firms did similar business.

It may not be out of place to mention here—though I do not think it a matter which rightly belongs to the penny plain, twopence coloured school—the efforts of the late Jack B. Yeats to revive the interest in the cult in the early days of the present century.

An enthusiastic lover of the toy theatre he drew and published through Elkin Mathews a number of original plays, including "Esmeralda," "The Treasure of the Garden," "The Scourge of the Gulph," "James Dance, or the Unfortunate Ship's Boy" and "James Flaunty, or the Terror of the Western Seas." They were all plays of a piratical and adventurous order and were beautifully drawn and coloured. They apparently did not meet with great success but they have a decided artistic attraction and some of the plays are rare. Copies coloured by the artist himself were sold at 5s. each. There was also a pantomime with the wonderful title of "The Mysterious Traveller, or the Gruesome Princess and the Pursuing Policeman." Possessors of these plays may count themselves as lucky.

Abroad children have been more or less constant to the cult of the toy theatre and in many countries the native equivalent of the cardboard drama has reached quite a high state of artistic perfection.

Most German toyshops can show you a variety of lithographed sheets of scenes and characters and a few may be obtained in France. The best that I have seen are produced by a Spanish firm in Barcelona. They are lithographed in tasteful colours on stout cardboard and reproduce the latest ideas in stage setting and with their illuminated transparencies look charming when set up. Czecho-Slovakia and Denmark too can show beautiful examples of settings for a toy stage which is planned on a far larger and grander scale than anything ever attempted in the history of our own Juvenile Drama. But notwithstanding the excellence of these foreign productions they lack for me that charm which the Webb and Pollock plays have preserved.

CHAPTER SEVEN

STEVENSON'S "POOR CUCKOO"

I SUPPOSE that in the literature of the Juvenile Drama—such as it is—there is no better known or more often quoted article than the essay "A Penny Plain and Twopence Coloured" by Robert Louis Stevenson.

I have read it again and again, each time with undiminished pleasure, and its phrases linger gratefully in the mind—" that shop which was dark and smelt of Bibles, was a lodestone rock for all who bore the name of boy "; " those pages of gesticulating

"THE EXTREME HARD FAVOUR OF ITS HEROINES"

villains, epileptic combats, bosky forests, palaces and warships, frowning fortresses and prison vaults—it was a giddy joy "; " the extreme hard favour of its heroines. . ."

These phrases, I say, are redolent of delight and to read them is to renew one's youth tenderly, deliciously, and perhaps a little sadly. These words were penned by an artist sensitive to the beauty of words. They were touched with a gentle humour and with something of the magic of the art he was appraising. He interpreted most surely the very spirit of the Juvenile Drama in all its fancy and extravagance.

Yet let us not be beguiled with the facile beauty of this charming piece of essay writing. The sad truth is that this famous and often quoted article enshrines a series of mis-statements, errors of fact, and a sad injustice; as a source of information to the curious it has caused widespread misapprehension. I have even read an article in which Webb was described as "an interloper"—on what grounds I cannot possibly imagine except that the writer had accepted all of Stevenson's statements.

In giving the term 'Skeltery' to the Juvenile Drama, and by his eulogy of Pollock at the expense of Webb, Stevenson performed a grave—and I am afraid deliberate—injustice which has been innocently perpetuated by many other writers.

It is not so much that Stevenson gave credit to Skelt for the achievement of others and ascribed to him virtues that he did not possess, but that he so unfairly tried to belittle Webb.

"It may be different with the rose but the attraction of this paper drama sensibly declined when Webb crept into the rubric, a poor cuckoo flaunting in Skelt's nest."

So wrote Stevenson and words more unjust were surely never penned.

The peculiar injustice of Stevenson's sneer lies in this: that his article, which originally appeared in *The Magazine of Art* in April 1884 when it was under the editorship of W. E. Henley, was illustrated with fifteen reproductions of prints ascribed by him to Skelt when as a matter of fact fourteen of them were taken from the original prints engraved by Webb himself. They were pictures from "The Miller and his Men" and "The Smuggler," two of the best of Webb's own productions. The fifteenth picture, a cavern scene, was the only one that could in any sense have been ascribed to Skelt. But Skelt himself was neither artist nor engraver, so even that was not the product of his personal hand or invention.

It has always mystified the experts that while using Webb's scenes and characters for the purpose of illustration Stevenson should have given nearly all the credit for the glory of the toy theatre to Redington or Pollock.

I have had the explanation from Mr H. J. Webb, son of William Webb, who well recalls the facts of the incident that led up to the writing of the essay. Here is the story in Mr Webb's own words: "One day Stevenson, who had very often come to our shop, told my father that he was going to write a history of the Juvenile Drama and said he wanted some pictures to illustrate it. My father then set about preparing some material and for several nights sat up writing what he knew about the subject.

"Some time later when Stevenson returned my father said: 'Here Mr Stevenson, where do I come in in this?' 'You don't come in at all, Mr Webb,' replied Mr Stevenson, 'I come in.'

"Naturally my father thought, as he had prepared the material, that he was going to share in the result. 'This won't do,' he said. 'I've helped with you in this history. Without me it would not be written. I have given you the information and besides you are using my pictures for the illustrations.'

SCENE FROM WEBB'S "HARLEQUIN JACK AND THE BEANSTALK"
It has been described as a masterpiece.

"But Stevenson stuck out. He said it was he who was writing the stuff and that unless he wrote it it would never be published.

"Then my father in anger said he would not allow him to use the material. He tore up what he had written and there was a fearful row in the shop. I can well remember it.

"As Mr Stevenson left he turned to my father and shaking his finger at him said: 'This is going to cost you something, Mr Webb; this is going to cost you a great deal.'

"And," concludes Mr Webb, "so it did."

These facts about Stevenson and the substance of the conversation were first revealed, I believe, by Mr Langley Levi, editor of *The Sunday Times,* Johannesburg, who visited Webb's shop when on holiday in England a few years ago and subsequently wrote a delightful article about the Juvenile Drama for his paper.

It was only recently—I am writing in 1932—that a controversy arose upon this matter and the pro-Webbs and pro-Pollocks angrily disputed in the sedate pages of *Notes and Queries*. One correspondent suggested that old Mr Webb's visitor must have been "some other Stevenson," and ridiculed the statement that the real R.L.S. was always "in and out of the shop" as Mr Webb had told an interviewer.

Mr H. J. Webb's retort to this was emphatic. Writing to *Notes and Queries* (June 6, 1931) he said that Stevenson visited his father's shop after his return from America at least three times to his knowledge. He was present on each occasion.

"I remember on one occasion," he wrote, "as he came in he noticed some of the coloured sheets hanging in the doorway and at once struck a theatrical attitude. After the quarrel the idea of the article was changed and being unable to get the necessary scenes and characters from my father R.L.S. obtained what he wanted from Clarke, who was an agent for the toy theatre.

"Skelt's prints are quite different from the illustrations for the article. In fact, when Clarke sold some of the plates for the toy theatre Skelt had given up business."

Undoubtedly Stevenson's article, whether it was written out of spite or not, has helped to create a legend, and I am afraid that the idea that Webb was an inferior figure in the history of the toy theatre and that Pollock was supreme will never be destroyed. Nine out of ten of the articles on the subject which continue to be written convey this suggestion.

Let it be understood, however, that the good Mr Pollock had no hand in this business himself; he is much too modest a gentleman for that. If he has profited a little out of the fame ascribed to him no one will surely begrudge it.

Personally, I think it is evident that Stevenson was aggrieved over Webb's refusal to supply him with material for his article. I believe Webb knew many secrets of the trade now for ever lost and his refusal must have been a sad blow for Stevenson, who is said to have contemplated writing a history of the subject. It is odd that Mr Webb did not seem to appreciate the value of the advertisement which Stevenson was prepared to give him in his article; the fault in the dispute was not entirely on one side.

Here it will be appropriate, I think, to examine the "poor cuckoo's" claim to fame.

I maintain that few men associated with the toy-theatre business deserve more honour than William George Webb, who went into the business in boyhood, remained in it for fifty-six years, and during that time produced more tinsel characters than any other man engaged in the trade, got out an admirable list of plays, and before his death managed to gather into his hands the bulk of the toy-theatre business.

Moreover, this distinction was his: apart from Park, whose apprentice he was, he was the only publisher who sketched, engraved, coloured, published and sold his own work.

In addition to this he wrote the books of half a dozen plays including "Robin

FRONTISPIECE FROM THE ORIGINAL PLAYBOOK OF WEBB'S "ROBIN HOOD"

Hood," "Aladdin," "The Miller and his Men," "The Battle of the Alma," and "The Battle of Inkerman."

"These books," wrote Mr Walter Hamilton in *Notes and Queries*, November 9, 1890, "were not only devoid of all vulgarity but were remarkable for the condensation of the leading incidents and dialogues."

And, says the same writer of the scenes and characters which Webb himself drew on the stone, "having in view the clientele he had to satisfy the costumes and architecture were singularly accurate and tasty. Of course the attitudes were stagey but seldom ungraceful."

Far from being a "poor cuckoo flaunting in Skelt's nest," then, Webb had every right to be regarded as a proud eagle rightfully occupying his own eyrie. Incidentally it was Webb's uncle, a gunsmith by trade, who was the first to make steel dies for the punching of tinsel ornaments for the embellishment of the single characters. Hence the trade that Webb built up in this particular line.

Webb was born in Surrey in 1819, the son of a prosperous London wool merchant, who carried on business in Crutched Friars. At the age of fourteen, having shown signs of artistic skill, he was, through the influence of an uncle engaged in the trade, bound as sole apprentice to Park, who was then carrying on a business as a printer and publisher of theatrical prints at 47 Leonard Street, Finsbury. He paid a premium of £60.

There he served for seven years, receiving no payment except a little pocket money, which he was given whenever he worked on Sunday. It was generally two-and-sixpence. He sketched and engraved for his master and was indeed a clever, promising, and industrious young pupil.

Webb's earliest work was contemporary with that of the later plays of Skelt, Park, and Green. Indeed some of Skelt's plays were drawn and engraved by him.

In 1838 he started in business on his own account at Ripley whither he returned, subsequently removing to Clothfair, then to Bermondsey Street, and later to 49 (afterwards 146) Old Street, St Luke's, not far from the present Webb shop (No. 124). His first wife, a cousin, had also been brought up in the trade and was an expert tinseller. She helped him considerably in his business.

He remarried on the death of his first wife and remained in business at Old Street until his death in 1890. He was in the business in the earliest days of the Juvenile Drama, had seen it progress, had personally known most of its leading publishers and had witnessed its decline and practical extinction. As a boy he often obtained sheets from West, Jameson, and Hodgson.

The old man appears to have taken the decay of the business quite philosophically. He attributed it partly to the increase of "cheap and nasty literature for boys" but chiefly to the home lessons which children at the period of his declining years had to study and which left them with little time and inclination for quiet, indoor pastimes.

Visited shortly before his death, when he was described as "a quiet old gentleman with eyes keen and bright," he said:

"Education has ruined the business, sir. Our children in these days neither have the patience nor the time necessary to colour and ornament the sheets. Besides photography has done away with the necessity for making careful drawings of our actors and nobody in these days would be satisfied with anything but a photographically correct likeness."

And he went on to muse thus:

"I am the last of them, there is not one living now! (This was not quite accurate as Pollock was, as now, still in the business). Ah, I can remember the palmy days of the business. I remember Skelt's, Lloyd's, and Jameson's and all the rest of them, but they are all gone. The plates of many of them are destroyed and the pictures can never be reproduced.

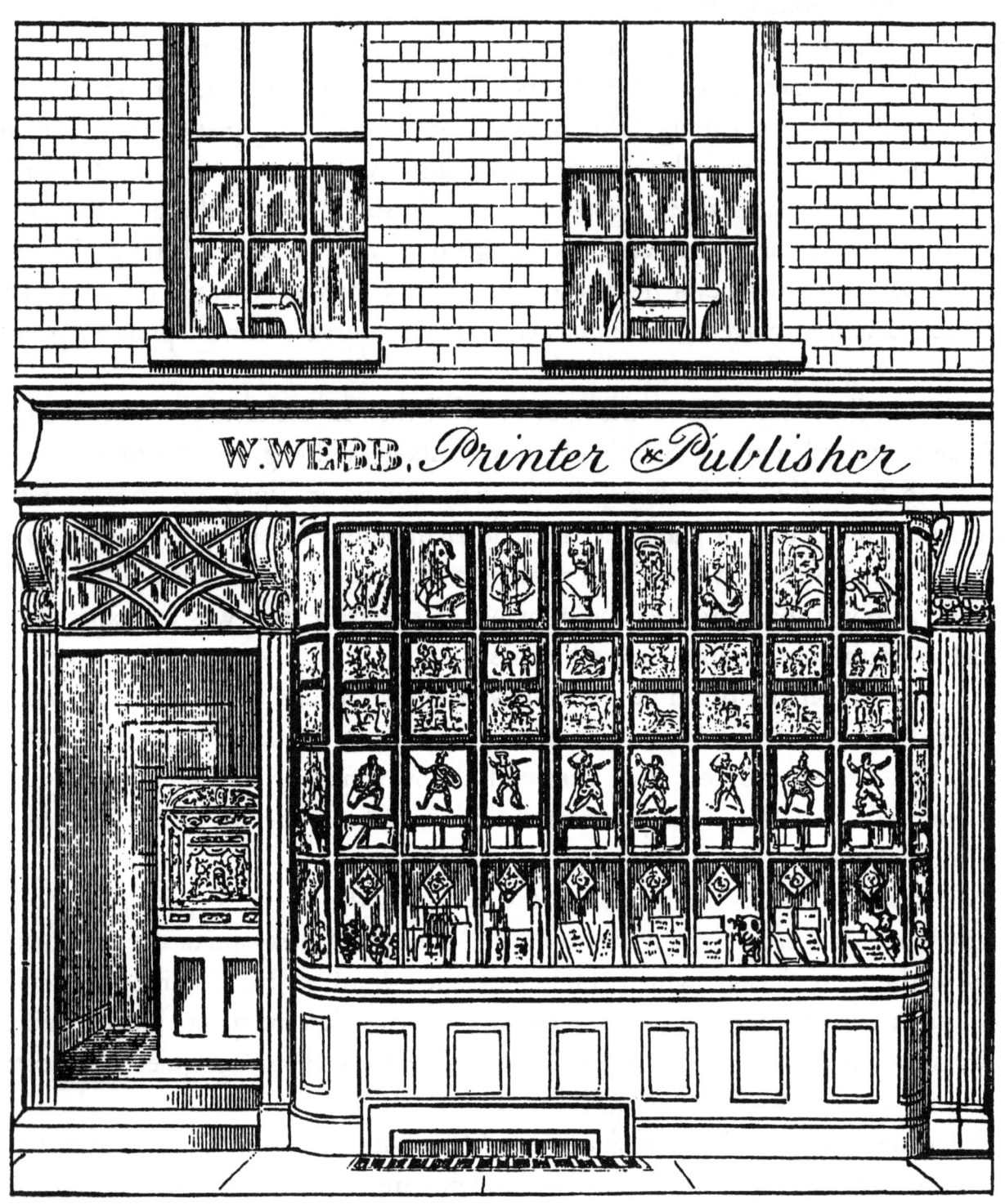

WEBB'S SHOP AT 49 OLD STREET, ST LUKE'S, REPRODUCED AS A SCENE IN "HARLEQUIN DAME CRUMP"

"When Skelt died he was in the workhouse and the artist who drew his pictures died there too.

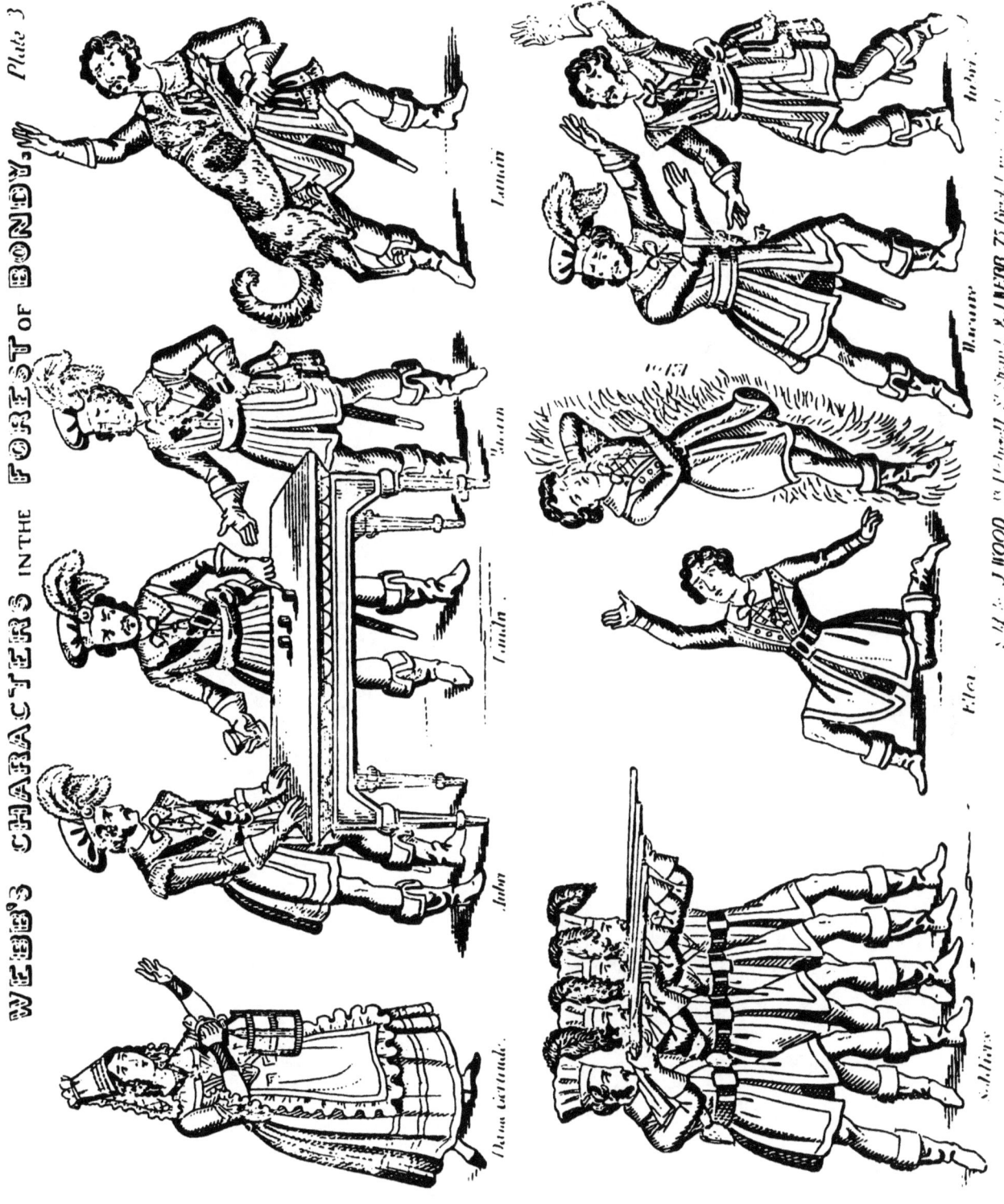

"His plates were bought up, some by me, some by Johnson, and those were laid by and were completely destroyed by rust. I have got a good few of the plates myself."

Mr Webb said that some of the characters in the plates were fair likenesses and some were not, for all the artists were not good.

"But still to me whenever I look at these old plates I can at once bring before me the characters themselves, so there must be some likeness."

Mr Webb produced to the interviewer a precious possession rarely revealed to the stranger. It was a huge book which he proudly described as being absolutely unique. There was not another like it, he said, and there never would be.

It was a ledger-like volume closely secured by a spring clasp, and it contained a complete selection of all the tinsel ornaments ever made—row upon row of tiny tinsel dots, swords, shields, hilts, helmets, glaives, gauntlets, buttons, belts, daggers, pistols, boots, feathers, and every possible kind of ornament, all arranged in marvellously neat array from one end of the great book to the other.

"That was my pattern book," he said. "It was made by my first wife while I was courting her. There never will be such another, for the dies are mostly destroyed and will never be made again."

I understand that this pattern book, the only one in existence and the envy of all collectors of tinselled portraits is now owned by a Surbiton publican who bought it, along with a collection of theatrical portraits from Harry Furniss's widow for £10. According to Mr H. J. Webb the face value of the tinsels contained in the book is over £100.

Webb's early plays were printed from copper, but as his business grew there was an enormous run on his sheets and the plates got so worn that the drawings had to be transferred to the lithographic stone.

"The plays produced by Webb," writes Dr Francis Eagle in *The Mask* (April 1913) "are second to none in artistry and craftsmanship and are of peculiar interest to this generation inasmuch as they illustrate for us some of the conventions, fads, and events during a greater part of the Victorian era . . . and were the last work of any importance issued in the Juvenile Drama."

An examination of the Webb prints will show that they were the work of a man with real skill and a taste for drawing and composition. Some of his scenes have real charm and delicacy of line. I like particularly his opening scene of "The Miller and his Men." His "Harlequin Jack and the Beanstalk, or the Good Little Fairies" has been described as a masterpiece. In this play Grimaldi's famous ditty "Hot Codlins" was directed to be sung. The pantomime embraced many tricks and changes of scene and allowed scope for some wonderful spectacular effects. According to Mr H. J. Webb this was the Drury Lane pantomime of 1860.

Webb specialized in plays of the patriotic type so popular at Astley's such as "The Battle of the Alma" and "The Battle of Waterloo." His "Union Jack," "Dred, or the Dismal Swamp," "The Rifle Volunteers"—a skit on the then prevalent craze—and the pantomime "Dame Crump" were also very popular.

"Robin Hood, or the Merry Men of Sherwood Forest"—which is not, as Stevenson suggested, one of Skelt's plays—is also notably good.

Webb's first play was "The Forest of Bondy," published in 1847; his last "The Hunter of the Alps," was published in 1880. This may be accounted as the last production of the real penny plain, twopence coloured school of art. There was no falling off in the quality of the workmanship and the main characteristics and style of figure, costume, and scene were preserved although this type of play was at the time of publication long out of date.

Stevenson figures so prominently in the Webb history that it will not be inappropriate to mention here that his failure as a dramatist is said to have been due to "The abiding influence of the toy theatre." These are the words of Sir Arthur Pinero who has pointed out that the pieces he attempted were planned in rivalry with "The Miller and his Men" and were therefore hopelessly out of date before they were conceived.

"Stevenson's early love of the toy theatre, no doubt, was responsible for the volume of plays which he wrote in conjunction with Henley," says another writer. "These show Stevenson in a congenial mood indeed and expressing himself in a literary form which must have been dear to him.

"It is a curious thing that Stevenson himself, a master of dialogue when that form of expression played its part in the development of the story, should be so stilted and artificial when using dialogue for dramatic purposes."

FIRST SHEET FROM WEBB'S LAST PLAY (1880)

CHAPTER EIGHT

MAGIC IN HOXTON

NOW let us take a trip to Hoxton and neighbouring St Luke's. You beg to decline? You know something, then, of that dingy hinterland of North London with its roaring traffic, its grim and grey aspects of shabby warehouses, its squalid rows of decayed shops and upholstering establishments, its air of dust and neglect, its narrow, murky, and forbidding side-streets.

Unlovely, to be sure. Nevertheless I promise you that the visit will be worth while. If you have imagination there is magic, romance, and wonderment there. Have not famous folk trod those ugly streets in search of these things—a goodly if queerly-assorted company—Dickens, Charles Chaplin, G. K. Chesterton, Gordon Craig, Winston Churchill, the Sitwells, Gladys Cooper, Diaghileff of Russian Ballet fame, George R. Sims, Lupino Lane, and Robert Louis Stevenson among them?

What common purpose has taken them thither? The Juvenile Drama, of course.

Yes, here in the midst of this desert of dingy brick, cluttered roadways, and roaring traffic, are the shrines, oppressively modern, at which many who have memories of happy childhood in which devotion to the toy theatre forms a part, who have an interest in a queer, enthralling pursuit of other days, who pay homage to odd conceit, or whose love of the theatre prompts them to explore every manifestation of its activity have come to do reverence.

Yes, here is the Mecca of what Stevenson calls 'Skeltery' (I borrow the term for its comprehensive usefulness though, as I have shown, it perpetuates a name ill-applied and unjustly inappropriate).

It is a Mecca in which there are two shrines engaged in friendly rivalry and if the names of their two arch-priests or presiding geniuses do not evoke a responsive thrill I shall be very sorry indeed for you.

Webb and Pollock! The names stir the mind with memories of the delights of happy childhood. They are magic words indeed for all who have tasted the delights of the Juvenile Drama and who remember the indefinable charm of everything associated with it—its quaintness, its sheer theatricality, its rich redolence of a vanished age, its magic conjuration of the past as it actually looked to our forbears, its manifold attendant pleasures and excitements, the long cosy, industrious evenings by the fireside which were spent in the preparation of the grand performance that rarely came off. The names of Webb and Pollock evoke indescribable delight mingled with that tender regret that weaves itself around the memories of far-off days.

So to renew one's youth one should make the journey to a dingy, unlovely neighbourhood and visit the shops of Webb and Pollock—the only survivors of what once in the heyday of its fame was a multitude of publishers of the Juvenile Drama. They linger on, not as the resort of the eager child clutching in its hand its pence to squander on sheets of endless delight, but as storehouses of quaint relics of the Victorian age to which collectors, artists, and stage designers are mainly the only visitors.

First then, let us visit the shop of H. J. Webb, son of *the* W. G. Webb. You will find in him a real character and, in his way, a notability, for he is the only man alive who has been in the Juvenile Drama trade all his working life. He is now (1932) eighty years of age and he still carries on business at 124 Old Street, St Luke's.

As his father was apprenticed to Park in 1828 there is between them over a century of unbroken history in the trade and of the Webb business.

Any time you visit the neighbourhood you will find Mr Webb in his shop, or perchance you may find him in a corner behind the counter engaged in colouring his prints, which are still in demand by collectors.

It is a stationer's, newsagent's, and tobacconist's shop principally but on the facia you will see that Mr Webb indicates that he is also a provider of the Juvenile Drama, while in a corner you will find a display of toy stages, stage fronts, tinselled pictures, and sheets of characters displayed. What was once the main business is now, of course, only a side-line.

Like Mr Pollock, his only rival, Mr Webb is a quietly spoken, gentle-mannered old man and does not look nearly his age. Hence I conclude that there is some mellowing, beneficent influence about the purveying of the Juvenile Drama that keeps its magicians in perpetual youth.

Mr Webb owns a valuable collection of plays and relics of the toy theatre from the earliest days of its existence including splendid selection of Skelt, West, and Hodgson prints, and original drawings by the two Cruikshanks, and Heath, many rare playbooks and sheets and plays possessed by no other collector, and has a rich storehouse of memories and lore about his delightful trade. He is soaked in its tradition and he loves the sentiment of it. He will correct you gently but insistently with a slow, wise smile when you are mistaken about a date or a play or any fact connected with the history of the toy theatre.

He takes an artist's pride in the craft. He is a connecting link with its remote and mysterious past. He has known some of its eminent figures. He likes nothing better than to talk about it.

H. J. WEBB'S SHOP, 124 OLD STREET, E.C., AS IT IS TO-DAY

His collection will make the mouth of any other enthusiast water with envy. His shop is a veritable museum of the Juvenile Drama. One of its most interesting exhibits is a vast collection of tinsel-maker's dies. He has over 6,000 copper plates from which the characters and scenes were engraved. He has also original drawings and draft sketches of the plays as well as drawings for plays that were never issued.

I have often visited him and he has shown me treasures that few other customers have been privileged to see. To Mr Webb I owe much of the information (or clues thereto) that this book contains.

When he left school in 1866 Mr Webb was apprenticed to his father. He was never able to draw like his father but he did most of the other jobs in the business. He went into business on his own account after his apprenticeship. When his father died in 1890 the business went to the second Mrs Webb under whom it unfortunately declined. The stock was never kept up to date, and when Mr H. J. Webb took it over the trade was too far gone to recover its old prosperity.

"It never had a chance," says Mr Webb, with a melancholy shake of the head.

So he turns from the present aspect of the toy theatre trade to the glories of its past. He has some memory of its flourishing days, for he went into the trade at an early age and his father probably knew more about the history of it than any other man.

"As an apprentice my father used to call on publishers like West and Hodgson. He knew all the big publishers and he saw them all go.

"In his heyday his business was very flourishing. Why, I remember we employed four families to do the colouring. There must have been at least fifteen people engaged in the work. But, do you know, I could tell all their work apart. No two of them coloured alike. I could easily pick out the work of any individual colourist. Some of it was beautifully done. One man—he was so small that you could pick him up and put him under your arm—was a perfect artist."

It appears that at the time of which Mr Webb speaks Redington employed only one colourist, which gives some idea of the relative importance of the rival businesses.

Mr Webb well remembers Stevenson and, as I have already described, can clearly recall the famous quarrel. He was in the shop at the time when Stevenson made his dramatic threat—a gesture which seems to have been much in the style of the drama which Stevenson so much favoured.

"Up to the time of that quarrel," says Mr Webb, "Stevenson was a frequent visitor to the shop. He was very fond of my father's plays; indeed it was my father who used to supply the Edinburgh shop from which he bought his prints as a boy. He would talk for hours about the toy theatre in our shop."

Dickens too, was a frequent visitor in Mr Webb's early days. He recalls visits of the late Earl of Munster and of a Chancellor of the Exchequer whose name he cannot remember.

One of Mr Webb's pleasantest memories is of Mr Winston Churchill who, as a boy of fourteen or thereabouts, would, while a pupil at a Brighton school, either send for supplies of his favourite plays or would come to the shop and select them for himself.

"He was a jolly and impulsive lad," says Mr Webb, "and I shall never forget the way he would vault over my counter."

And now having visited Mr Webb let us see Mr Pollock, the only other survivor of the toy-theatre trade. You will find his shop at 73 Hoxton Street not far away. Strange that the tide of popularity receding from the old pastime, should have left these survivors stranded in the same unlikely district. How came it that this was the soil upon which the trade last flourished? I cannot tell, but there is something not inappropriate in the setting in which one now finds these two old businesses. They are reminders of the London of Dickens's day and the surroundings are now Dickensian in the extreme. Particularly the shop of Benjamin Pollock. You will find it some way up Hoxton Street near what was once the famous "Old Brit" theatre, home of melodrama and pantomime and now, alas! a cinema.

It is a quaint little, low-fronted shop with its windows divided into small square panes. It is just as it has stood for about a hundred years and the surroundings cannot have much altered in that time. It is dim and dingy, but peer through those windows and you will see a storehouse of magic and delight.

There is a little stock of stationery, toys, and oddments but what attracts the attention is a large model stage, glaringly coloured with a full setting of an early pantomime.

CHARACTERS IN POLLOCK'S "CORSICAN BROTHERS"

It is a transformation scene aglitter with tinsel and the stage is crowded with little cardboard characters. And the little stage is set with sheets of scenes and characters of the

POLLOCK'S "NEW AND IMPROVED DROP SCENE"

"THE OLD CURIOSITY SHOP OF THE JUVENILE DRAMA"
73 Hoxton Street.

many plays famous in the history of the toy theatre—"Paul Clifford," "The Maid and the Magpie," "The Corsican Brothers," "Oliver Twist"—yes, and of course, "The Miller and his Men."

Enter the shop, but if you are tall and there is anything hanging from the ceiling be careful not to bump your head. Stevenson did so fifty years or so ago, the proprietor will proudly tell you.

It is a small, low-ceilinged shop, dim, mysterious, and altogether alluring. It smells strangely but not unpleasantly of musty paper, of glue, and of resinous wood. Behind the counter are rows upon rows of neatly arranged little boxes, each one devoted to the complete sheets of one play. There is a big glass case in the corner in which there are more plays and stage fronts. Round about the walls are framed tinsel pictures of theatrical favourites of the past limned in belligerent and heroic attitudes. The ceiling is studded with hooks. Once upon a time in the good old days completed stages hung from them. Now they are vacant. Eloquent commentary upon the decay of a noble trade!

Such is the old curiosity shop of the drama.

A pleasant faced, gentle-mannered man comes out of the parlour workshop to greet you; it is Benjamin Pollock, no less, the very B. Pollock referred to by Stevenson in the famous essay.

Mr Pollock is now seventy-five years of age and he will talk in strains not unmingled with melancholy, though with gentle resignation, about the glory and romance of the trade which was already in its decline when he was a young man.

"Toy stages are too slow for the modern boy and girl," he said when I last saw him. "Why, my own grandchild isn't interested in them. Children were more painstaking in the old days than they are now."

In the old days things were indeed different.

"Orders all the year round," says Mr Pollock. "In the autumn we began to get really busy. I had several outdoor men working for me then and we would often send off half a gross of wooden stages on one order. I had one man who would come in just to do the woodwork for the stages. I was kept busy in turning out the lithographed plates, others would help in the colouring and my wife would serve in the shop.

"Nowadays I can do the whole job myself. One Christmas I didn't sell a single stage."

Still Mr Pollock has frequently to execute orders from abroad. He has sent stages to Lupino Lane, the comedian, in America, and to Egypt of all unlikely places. When last I called upon him he had just completed a handsomely set stage for the Sitwell family.

Penny plain, twopence coloured is only a phrase now. You have to pay more than that though the sheets are still cheap as curiosities go. A full set of Pollock's "The Miller and his Men" costs 3s. 8d. if you buy it coloured. The most elaborate production, the pantomime of "Sleeping Beauty" is 7s. 8d. Or you can get "Charles the Second" for the knock-down price of 1s. 8d. The colourings, put on in some cases forty years ago, are as brilliant and as startling as ever.

You can buy a neatly-made little stage, constructed to fold up compactly, with a curtain to roll, grooves for the wings and tin footlights a few complete for a few shillings.

I looked over Mr Pollock's stock stowed away in their neat little compartments and selected some of my favourite plays. It is thrilling to come across all the big names and characters with their preposterous heroic attitudes, their oddly unattractive heroines and the strange scenes of melodrama and pantomime. "Timour the Tartar," "The Maid

SCENE IN POLLOCK'S "THE BATTLE OF WATERLOO"

and the Magpie," "The Battle of Waterloo." What treasures! They are to be handled like the rarest of old prints. One savours them and lingers over them fondly and reverently.

Mr Pollock has been in the business for over fifty years and his connection with it began with a love romance. Before he entered the business he was engaged in the fur trade.

BENJAMIN POLLOCK IN HIS SHOP
Note the stage and the character in tin slide.

He took over the shop lock, stock, and barrel from Redington its founder. He took more—he married pretty Miss Redington. Gordon Craig has told the story very charmingly in *The Mask*. He says:

> The one who excelled in this art (*i.e.*, tinselling) was little Miss Redington. She was so delightful that she turned the heads of the young men who worked for papa.
> At last one passionate admirer realising that if this sort of thing went on much longer the ancient and novel art of theatre-making would die out, seized the bull by the horns and demanded of Mr Redington the hand of his daughter.
> This man was B. Pollock, the only surviving man of the old school of ancient theatrical art. He married pretty Miss Redington and in time changed the name of the shop from Redington to Pollock.

Mr Pollock, though, is not as Mr Craig says—this is only one example of the influence of the Stevenson-made legend—"the only surviving man" in this trade; but let this pretty little record of a pretty romance stand.

Mr Pollock has carried on the business ever since 1877 when Redington died. He has had many notable customers in his time. Americans visit him, so do many literary and stage folk. "Ellen Terry once bought a stage here," he is fond of telling. "Her son, Gordon Craig, has often been to see me." He is very proud of the fact that the Russian ballet under Diaghileff used some of his plates for the design of their ballet "The Triumph of Neptune" some years ago.

He tells too of visits of Gladys Cooper and Charles Chaplin, of Lew Lake, and of Lupino Lane whose great aunt was Mrs Sarah Lane of the 'Old Brit' near by. As a boy Lupino Lane used to play about the neighbourhood and was a constant purchaser of the plays.

But Mr Pollock is proudest of all that among his customers was Stevenson. He will point to you the exact spot where the lanky Scotsman stood when he historically banged his head against the toy stage half a century ago and provided him with his proudest reminiscence.

"Oh yes, he would always bump his head in that way," says Mr Pollock. "I remember him quite well although it was so long ago. He was a gentleman who never said much. I can remember that he was always pale and ill-looking and he was always most interested in plays about pirates and highwaymen."

And that is about all that Mr Pollock has to say about Stevenson, who seems to have taken his pleasures very gravely.

"It is a long time since anyone in this district gave a farthing show in his coal cellar," says Mr Pollock, talking about the once flourishing times, "But I still get a few elderly customers. It was only the other day that a City gentleman drove up here in a car and bought a selection of plays. He said he had collected them as a boy. We get several customers like that. They are still fond of the old pastime and that is a thing that the young ones can't understand.

"Practically all my stock has been here fifty years or so. There's enough to last out my time, I reckon. I still have all the old plates and the lithographic stones, but I do not have to use them much for fresh prints although I still do the colouring in the summer time when trade is slacker. The stones which weigh a goodish bit used to come in handy to steady the shop during the war-time air raids."

Strange destiny that must have considerably astonished the gentle shade of the good Mr Redington!

You can still see the old press off which the prints were taken in the little back room. It is a quaint curiosity, and dust-covered though it is and rusty looking, it is still capable of good work if it should ever be required again. But there is little likelihood of that, for Mr Pollock's sons have gone in for more remunerative work. When he is gone there will be no one to carry on this ancient business. The famous firm of Redington and Pollock will then be a legend.

CHAPTER NINE

STAGE HISTORY IN MINIATURE

IF they had no artistic or other pictorial interest the sheets of the Juvenile Drama would still be worthy of study to anyone concerned with the history of the British stage. They provide a valuable document of the past.

"Their value rests mainly on the fact that we have here the only delineations of the actors, dresses, and scenery of many famous plays in the first half of the nineteenth century," says one writer in protest against the fact that "they are much despised by superior persons."

We know how much were the pains taken to ensure accuracy in reproducing plays in miniature, and it may therefore be agreed that these little sheets afford a record of what theatrical productions were like a hundred years or more ago, and of the old fashions and conventions, such as we do not otherwise possess. It is a complete picture of the British theatre as it was and of a kind that has ceased to exist. From such material as this alone a complete history of the stage in the early part of the last century might be composed.

The very appearance of the old theatres such as Drury Lane, the Lyceum, Covent Garden, and the 'Old Brit,' at Hoxton is reproduced in the penny and twopenny stagefronts issued by different publishers. They give us an excellent idea of what the interiors looked like and of the changes that have come about in the design of stage and proscenium and of the old ideas of what constituted luxury and grandeur.

In *Thirty-Five Years of an Author's Life* published in 1859 Edward Fitzball, the dramatist who wrote "The Pilot" and other favourite plays of the time which were reproduced in miniature in the days of the Juvenile Drama, says:

> They (the minor theatres) have risen to a pitch of grandeur and excellence little or never anticipated by old stagers. The theatres in their interior became so magnificent as to elicit both wonder and astonishment; the Surrey Theatre at one time being decorated with gold and velvet, a Genoa velvet curtain covering the stage.
>
> The Coburg, patronised by Her Royal Highness, the lamented Princess Charlotte, and Prince Leopold was decorated with one sunny glitter of gold and pretty mirrors with a superb looking glass curtain which drew up and let down in the sight of the audience reflecting every form and face in the gorgeous house.

But even this glowing and rhapsodical description hardly gives us so graphic an idea as one of the West or Webb or Redington prosceniums which were sold for one penny or twopence.

I have before me one of Redington's stage fronts; I think it is a reproduction of the proscenium of the Britannia Theatre in the day when it flourished as a home of the drama and pantomime in the earlier half of the last century.

It is a stately affair in the heavy classical style. Across the top of the proscenium arch is a panel depicting a Roman chariot careering through the thick woolly clouds. The ambitious youth who chose to 'build up' his stage could place above it some additional panels of classic design, the whole to be tastefully surmounted with a bust of Shakespeare.

Below there are three panels representing respectively, a knight's tourney, St George and the Dragon, and William Tell shooting the apple off his son's head. From the streaky appearance of the proscenium pillars one supposes that they represent marble. There are clusters of lamps, for this was Thespis of the gas or oil age. There are four boxes with the customary proscenium doors below.

These doors are a very interesting reminder of an old convention in theatre design. In the early part of the nineteenth century every proscenium had doors on either side resembling in every way the front doors of a house, complete with door-knob and knocker. When taking their calls the actors would appear through one of the doors, cross the stage, and make their exit by the other. These proscenium doors were generally coloured green. They practically disappeared from the stage about a hundred years ago. In the old theatres the footlights were just as prominently in view as they were in the toy replicas. The shaded lamps continued to show themselves unabashed until as late as 1854.

The 'built up' stage fronts show the survival of the old 'apron' stage just as it had persisted since Elizabethan days. There was ample room for the actor to strut and declaim in front of the boxes where much of the action took place.

The sheets of characters are a portrait gallery of old favourites in miniature.

In *London's Lost Theatres* Errol Sherson writes:

> Many of the characters were actual portraits of famous actors of the time. The St George was Ducrow of Astley's. The Red Rover was Yates of the Adelphi and another character in " Red Rover " was a portrait of T. P. Cooke, the original Martin Truefold in the famous Surrey drama " True to the Core " and the well-known William in " Black-eyed Susan." In " The Bottle Imp " the picture of Willibald is a likeness of Oxberry.
> Claudine in Cruikshank's " Miller and his Men " was probably a portrait of Sally Booth who created the part in the play, and the character of Ravina was also a portrait of a very famous actress of her day but whom I have been unable to identify.

Examine some of the West or Hodgson sheets and you will clearly see the likenesses of Munden and Liston, the famous comedians, exactly as they appeared in many of their

LISTON AND FARLEY AS KARL AND GRINDOFF IN WEST'S "THE MILLER AND HIS MEN"

famous parts. As Lamb wrote, "There is one face of Farley, one face of Knight, one —but what a face it is!—of Liston."

The chubby features and the retroussé nose of Liston are faithfully reproduced in West's "The Miller and his Men" and so are the heavier features of Farley who was the first of the Grindoffs.

The plates, too, afford us an excellent idea of stage dressing in those far-off days. Our predecessors were less advanced in this respect apparently than they were in the matter of scenic design. Some of the figures look very quaint and comic to our eyes. In Hodgson's "Macbeth," for instance, Macbeth and Macduff wore the gigantic feathered bonnets, such as were worn by Scottish regiments of that time; they were then thought quite appropriate to the period of the play.

"On the living stage fifty years ago," remarks John Ashton in *Varia*, "accuracy of costume was not so much studied as now. So in the mimic drama there is a great sameness: the ladies generally wore high-waisted dresses of the Regency and the beaux had only advanced as far as pantaloons."

I have indicated elsewhere how the toy stage reflects the current taste in plays over that period of the British stage in which drama was at its lowest ebb. All the favourite plays were of violent action and of crude plot or else they partook of unashamed sentiment and robustious patriotism. The sentiments were naive, frank, and simple; the speeches were rhetorical and stilted. The humour was inconceivably silly and poor. The sheets of characters reflect the favoured style of acting. It must have been of the Crummles kind, full of bold action, large and expressive gestures, violent stampings, and general exaggeration and little restraint.

The sheets are most valuable of all as a record of scene-painting and designing.

Really the art of scene-painting was more advanced a century or so ago than most people are inclined to realise and some of the sets must have looked quite picturesque and charming on the stage, although the absence of adequate stage lighting must have been a considerable handicap.

It was the day of unabashed realism; a tree was not ashamed to look like a tree and not like an isosceles triangle, as is to-day very often the tendency, nor were velvet curtains deemed a suitable background for the romantic drama or for depicting the magnificences and pageantry of Shakespeare.

The woodland sets with which the Juvenile Drama abounds show that the scene-painters of old excelled particularly in the depiction of luxuriant foliage and arboreal compositions. In the interior sets our ancestors were perhaps not so far advanced. They were content with the simple backcloth and side wings. Often the backcloth bore painted representations of furniture on it.

None of the toy theatre plays employs the 'box' setting for domestic scenes. That, I believe, did not come into vogue until Bancroft and Marie Wilton brought realism to the stage in their little theatre in Tottenham Street in the days when the toy theatre was waning in popularity.

Many notable plays of the past will be found pictured completely for our benefit in the toy drama. Here are some of the most interesting of them with the theatres and dates of their production:

"The Miller and his Men"	(I. Pocock)	Covent Garden	October 21, 1813
"Black-eyed Susan"	(D. Jerrold)	The Surrey	June 8, 1829
"Casco Bay"	(W. Bayle Barnard)	Olympic	December 3, 1827
"Cataract of the Ganges"	(W. T. Moncrieff)	Drury Lane	October 27, 1823
"Jack Sheppard"	(J. C. Buckstone)	Adelphi	October 28, 1839
"Oliver Twist"	(Edward Sterling)	Adelphi	February 25, 1839
"Olympic Revels"	(J. R. Planche and Dance)	Olympic	January 8, 1831
"Paul Clifford"	(Ben Webster)	Coburg	March 12, 1832
"The Pilot"	(Edward Fitzball)	Adelphi	October 31, 1825
"Uncle Tom's Cabin"		Standard	September 13, 1852

In some of the plays there are scenes picturing actual localities affording an agreeable glimpse of the topography of London a century ago. One of the most interesting is Hodgson's "Life in London." It is undated but to judge by the drawing it must have been issued some time in the thirties. Its many scenes provide an interesting panorama of London at that period and of the places where the 'fast life' was led.

There are glimpses of the Burlington Arcade, Tattersall's, Almack's, Cribb's Parlour, Temple Bar (when the archway stood in Fleet Street), Fleet Street (which seems then to have consisted mainly of prison-like structures of grim aspect) and Leicester Square

SOME OF BAILEY'S PANTOMIME CHARACTERS
From the British Museum Collection

which was, as this scene shows it before its reclamation by Baron Grant, all railings, cobbles, and lamp-posts.

One service which the Juvenile Drama is able to render is to convey to us a graphic idea of what the old form of pantomime was like. Excellent examples of its characters will be found in the sheets of Bailey and Skelt.

The pantomime as we know it now is little akin to the kind of entertainment that reached the height of its popularity in the days of Grimaldi a hundred years or so ago. According to some authorities pantomime was introduced into England by Mr Rich, manager of the Covent Garden Theatre, the first entertainment of the kind being produced at Lincoln's Inn Fields Theatre. It is more likely, however, that the first pantomime was that produced by a Shrewsbury dancing-master named Weaver in 1702. One of his pantomimes "The Loves of Mars and Venus" met with great success. The arrival in London in 1717 of a troupe of French pantomimists with the additional attraction of performing dogs gave this kind of entertainment an impetus and the Grimaldis, father and son, further developed and popularised it.

Pantomime owes much to and was a development of the *Commedia dell' Arte* of Italy, whence come its characters of clown, pantaloon, harlequin, and columbine. Grimaldi, the greatest of all pantomime performers that the English stage has ever known, and who figured so often in the penny plain, twopence coloured sheets, perfected the pantomime and made it peculiarly British and national in character. No other country has known anything like this particular form of entertainment. The clown as we know him now—or at least as he was known until some years ago, for the character has now almost disappeared from the stage—was practically the creation of Grimaldi. It was he who originated his peculiar gait and his voice and who invented much of the traditional business.

In the pantomimes of old the pranks of clown and harlequin were an integral and indeed the most important part of the performance. Indeed they were woven into the fabric of the story instead of being relegated, as they were later in the development of the pantomime, to the end of the performance, where they made a perfunctory appearance before a drop scene or advertisement curtain and disappeared after a few minutes' horseplay with sausages and red-hot poker.

Clown and pantaloon and the rest of the characters of the harlequinade were the leading figures of the pantomime story proper transformed by harlequin's magic bat. Harlequin was the hero of the piece, as most of the titles indicate. The heroine you would find changed into tripping columbine; the bold, bad baron would become pantaloon, and so forth. These metamorphoses would take place during the Grand Transformation Scene. Hence its name and oft-forgotten purpose.

It was a singular, unsophisticated form of entertainment, as a study of the sheets in conjunction with the playbooks and the *Memoirs of Grimaldi* (edited by Boz) will show. Indeed a vast number of the plays and pantomimes mentioned in the life of the great clown will be found in the sheets of the Juvenile Drama. Among such entertainments, in all of which Grimaldi took part, frequently with his friend Bologna, famous as harlequin, were the pantomimes "Dulce Domum," "Harlequin and Blue Beard," "Harlequin and the Forty Virgins" (all at Sadler's Wells), "The Golden Fish," "Mother Goose," and "Harlequin and the Swans" (Covent Garden), and the Covent Garden plays of "Pizarro," "La Perouse," "Raymond and Agnes," "Valentine and Orson," "Aladdin," and "Cherry and Fair Star." Some of these pieces are of an extraordinary simplicity and naiveté but it is probable that they owed much of their success to their Oriental pageantry.

All these plays you will find pictured in the toy-theatre sheets with the processions of pantomime giants, 'big-heads,' ogres, and other fearful wild-fowl of the time. You will not, however, find in them a sign of the strapping principal boy, all tights and ostrich feathers. That important personage was a later development of the pantomime introduced after the wane of the toy theatre's popularity and was probably the cause of the clown's decline in importance.

The old-time Harlequinade was pursued through many scenes. Clown cracked his jests and performed his practical jokes in front of drop scenes that largely represented humble shopping thoroughfares. There sausages could be stolen from the butcher's, butter slides prepared in front of the grocer's, huge caddies purloined from the tea merchants, and so forth. On the facias of these shops would be inscribed the names of the occupiers, embodying puns of an excruciating kind.

A great feature of the old Harlequinades and one of its chiefest delights were the 'tricks'—the magic changes of scene and objects performed at the touch of Harlequin's bat. Thus a bed would be transformed into a horses' drinking trough, a corpulent drunkard into a barrel, a pig into a load of sausages, a gigantic egg into an equally huge rooster, and so forth. Or in the twinkling of an eye the appearance of a quiet shop front would change to the confusion of clown and his associates.

These 'tricks' were performed by the aid of falling flaps of scenery—a primitive device no doubt, but one which commanded the wonderment and admiration of the pantomime-goer of old.

Sheets of "tricks" were supplied by all the toy-theatre dealers and they were also sold ready-made for the convenience of the unskilled youth. West's sheets of pantomime tricks (some of which I have reproduced) were particularly good and some of them were excellently drawn.

The pantomime sheets studied in conjunction with Boz's *Grimaldi* will give one a vivid idea of what the old-time pantomime was like.

A POLLOCK STAGE SET WITH THE TRANSFORMATION SCENE IN "THE SILVER PALACE"

CHAPTER TEN

"THE MILLER AND HIS MEN"

Now let us look at "The Miller and his Men," that classic which transcends in popularity all the plays of the Juvenile Drama.

For more than half a century the popularity of this cardboard thriller endured in spite of all changes in price and fashion. Skelt alone published five versions of the piece (one of which was probably Dyer's) and when Brett issued it in 1874 it was one of the last of the penny plain plays to be published.

Writing in *The Era* Almanac in 1891 Theo Arthur says:

> An edition of the popular "Miller and his Men" was published by every firm so that you could have a chubby, hideous, or arabesque Claudine (the heroine) according to your taste and undoubtedly the "Miller and his Men" was sold in the proportion of twenty to one of all the other plays.

That the toy theatre can be said to exist now or to be known at all is largely because of its association with this ancient, romantic play. Its very title is enough to conjure up at once a vision of the toy theatre in all its glory of our youth and to set the heart longing for lost delights.

"The Miller and his Men" was one of the many English imitations written under the influence of German romanticism represented in fiction by the lurid novels of Mrs Radcliffe. It was, of course (as William Archer in *The Old Drama and the New* points out) only the worse elements that proved capable of transplantation.

In French's Standard Drama acting editions the play is described as a melodrama in two acts by Isaac Pocock, a prolific but long forgotten dramatist who wrote, among other plays, "The Robber's Wife," "John of Paris," "Hit or Miss," "Robinson Crusoe," and "The Magpie and the Maid," which also figures in the Juvenile Drama.

This famous "melo-drama" was first produced at Covent Garden Theatre on October 21, 1813 as an 'afterpiece' to "Venice Preserv'd" when Farley played the villain Grindoff and Liston, the comedian, Karl. Special music was composed for the production by Bishop, and his airs are described as being "quaint and pleasant."

The piece was got up, according to one account "with splendid liberality," the acting was described as excellent, and the reception was brilliant. It had the splendid advantage of a sensational end. Says a writer of the period: "A piece with an explosion is sure to go off well; and many an author can bear grateful testimony that, when deserted by genius, he has been saved by gunpowder." Alas! the modern playwright has no such easy resource.

Of the first production the dramatic critic of *The Times* on October 22 wrote (after complaining of the late hour at which the performance closed) as follows:

> Suffice it to state then that *The Miller and his Men* are a gang of robbers and their chief which infests a wood in Bohemia maintaining meanwhile ostensibly reputable characters. This is most improbable and and so are all the incidents of the piece; yet there are situations in it not devoid of effect. The thieves are detected in their attempt to carry off the cottager's daughter whose lover had previously entered himself in their gang with a view to discovering their haunts and frustrating their plots and by him she is rescued from the cave of the ravishers. The piece then concludes with a firework so splendid that it might well represent CACUS in his den. This, of course, calls forth peals of approbation; and *The Miller and his Men* was given out for a second representation amidst great applause. Liston is in the stale service representing a servant more fond of eating than of working.

FRONT PAGE OF WEBB'S BOOK OF WORDS

And this is what *The Morning Post* had to say about it:

> A new Melo-Drama from the pen of Mr Pocock called *The Miller and his Men* was the afterpiece. It is necessary for us to say very few words on the subject of this entertainment; it is made

up of the usual melo-dramatic ingredients, *viz.*, thunder and lightning, bewildered travellers, hospitable cottagers, and jolly robbers. Mr Pocock has used these with skill and produced a piece which possesses some portion of interest and yields considerable amusement. To look for probability in a Melo-Drama would be almost as ridiculous as to seek it in a Harlequinade; and to complain of the unnatural exclamations of its heroes no less unreasonable than it would be to denounce the blunders of the Clown as things which cannot be and therefore ought not to be pictured. The Miller and his men are guilty of many extravagances; some of the incidents which occur are poor but an agreeable bustle is kept up from the beginning of the piece to its end. Several of the situations are good and the *explosion* of a mill at the conclusion treating the audience with a *blow-up* made it *go off* with boundless *éclat*.

The scenery is particularly beautiful. The music by Mr Bishop is pleasing and appropriate; and the acting throughout is good.

Although the play is generally attributed to Pocock the actual authorship is a matter of dispute.

I have read that shortly before the date of the production a poor hack author named Lyons sent to the management of Covent Garden a number of plays among which was a drama entitled "Robbers of the Rhine." The play was shortly afterwards returned to him along with the rest, but subsequently "The Miller and his Men" was produced and the unfortunate Lyons then found that the plot of this melodrama had been taken from his play.

It appears that in those days unfortunate authors of this kind had no redress against piracy.

When one reads through the condensed versions of this play prepared for the toy theatre its literary and dramatic merit does not appear to be very high, yet listen to what one eminent modern critic has to say about the play and those of its kind that were so popular during this period of stage history. It is Dr Brander Matthews, writing in *Scribner's Magazine* in October 1915:

> The special form of melodrama that flourished in the later years of the eighteenth century and the earlier years of the nineteenth century deserves a more careful study than it has yet received. Apparently it was due partly to the decadence of the native type of drama represented by George Lillo's "George Barnwell" and partly to the stimulation received from the emotional pieces of the German Kotzebue and from the picturesque pieces of the French Pixrecourt. And not to be neglected is the influence immediately exerted on the popular plays of the later part of that period covered by the vogue of the romances of Scott and Cooper.
>
> Although these plays were devoid of literary merit, of style, of veracity, of character delineation, of sincerity of motive, they were not without theatrical effectiveness or they could never have maintained themselves in the theatre.
>
> As Sir A. Pinero has seen clearly a drama which was sufficiently popular to be transformed to the toy stage was almost certain to have a sort of rude merit in its construction. The characterisation would be hopelessly conventional, the dialogue bald and despicable—but the situations would be artfully arranged, the story adroitly told and with spirit.

These ingenious and ingenuous pieces were not contributions to the English national drama and they were not enshrined in its annals but they were effective stage plays nevertheless and they had therefore an essential quality lacking in the closet dramas that Shelley and Byron were composing in those same years.

When West first issued "The Miller and his Men" he soon had to endure the competition of editions of that piece published by his rivals in the trade—Hodgson, Jameson, Kenilworth, Smart, Marks, and others.

The play enjoyed popularity in the real theatre for some years but when in the 'sixties Buckstone attempted to revive it at the Haymarket the experiment was not a success. A proposed revival at the now demolished Elephant & Castle Theatre a few years ago, to my grief, came to nothing! As a dramatic curiosity and done in the old-fashioned full-blooded manner it would surely have been interesting. Perhaps some day the play will appeal to Sir Nigel Playfair; it would make a capital Christmas entertainment.

Because of its associations with the toy theatre the play was a particular favourite of Charles Dickens.

He produced it while he was a pupil at Wellington House Academy, Hampstead Road. In Forster's *Life of Charles Dickens* Dr Henry Danson, a fellow pupil, recalls how Dickens and his friends delighted in toy theatricals. He says:

> We mounted small theatres and got up very gorgeous scenery to illustrate "The Miller and his Men," and "Cherry and Fair Star." I remember the present Mr Beverley, the scene-painter, assisted us in this. Dickens was always the leader in these plays, which were occasionally presented with much solemnity before an audience of boys and in the presence of the ushers.
>
> My brother, assisted by Dickens, got up "The Miller and his Men" in a very gorgeous form. Master Beverley constructed the mill for us in such a way that it could tumble to pieces with the assistance of crackers. At one representation the fireworks in the last scene ending with the destruction of the mill were so very real that the police interfered and knocked violently at the doors.

Dickens's after-taste for theatricals might have had its origin in these small affairs.

"Anyone familiar with the old *Household Words* will recall the many allusions to this old play" wrote Dickens's old friend Percy Fitzgerald in *The Dickensian* (March 1908).

"This good, old crusted piece was . . . revived in 1835 just as Boz was devoting himself to the stage. It was thus that he ever thought fondly of and cherished all the varied images of that happy time. Sometimes with a merry twinkle in his eye he would strike off with the words with which the piece opens: 'More sacks for the mill.'"

Fitzgerald tells how John Hollingshead revived the play "under absurd conditions" with the idea of refuting the notion that all the old pieces were good pieces—apparently on the lines of the modern Gate Theatre burlesqued revivals of early Victorian pieces.

SCENE FROM WEST'S "THE MILLER AND HIS MEN"
Dated July 3, 1828.
From the British Museum Collection

So Dickens and Fitzgerald went to a performance at Drury Lane with high expectations of renewing old delights.

"Then," writes Fitzgerald,

came the glee "When the wind blows, then the mill goes" to Bishop's old-fashioned strains execrably performed, as indeed was the whole. The players and their diction was exaggerated, the old-fashioned spectacle became a burlesque. Alas! the whole was stupid, dull and heavy to a degree so at last about the second act Boz arose slowly and sadly and said he could stand it no longer. I really think he was grieved at having his ideal shattered and perhaps mortified.

I suppose nearly every collector or anyone living who ever owned a toy theatre has seen the Pollock and Webb versions of the play.

Webb's edition was reproduced from the last production of the piece in London which took place at the Princess's Theatre in Oxford Street, and it appears to differ in many respects from the details of the play as published by West, Lloyd, Skelt, and Green. For one thing it introduced a grand ballet of "zingari."

"GRAND BALLET OF ZINGARI" IN WEBB'S "THE MILLER AND HIS MEN"

Indeed I give the palm to Webb, for his version of the blowing-up of the mill which was the crowning excitement of this grand melodrama is more lurid, imaginative, and affrighting than any other version I have seen. There are more disjointed bodies and flying timbers than in any of the rival publications' pictures of this scene. Upon it the artist lavished an opulent imagination.

Was there ever indeed such an opportunity for lurid spectacle as this play provides? Was there ever such an excuse for the sacrificial burning of one's pocket money in pyres of red fire?

And what play is so full of whiskered, stare-eyed banditry, deeds of darkness and noble sentiment?

"The Miller and his Men" is an exciting drama about a robber band posing as harmless, well-floured millers so as to carry on their devilish pursuits unsuspected. The setting is in Bohemia, the period the beginning of the nineteenth century. The scenery is of nature in its most luxuriant and extravagant mood embellished by man with great

A 'CUT-OUT' SCENE IN WEBB'S "THE MILLER AND HIS MEN"

floridity of architecture. That nobly-planned castle that crowns the summit of the hill in Webb's version and upon which the sun sheds rays of splendour unparalleled has always been one of my favourite scenes.

The costumes may be Bohemian of that period but they seem to belong rightly to no clime, nation, or time particularly. Even in the meanest character they are luxurious, and the tight breeches of the male characters reveal a manly array of calf, knee, and thigh. One cannot, however, extend much praise for the beauty of the women-folk. However, the virtue of the heroines was unassailable, and that should satisfy.

The play itself is full of desperate encounters, fierce combats, and much sword-play and plentiful carousing. There is, too, a modicum of love affair and of sentimental business.

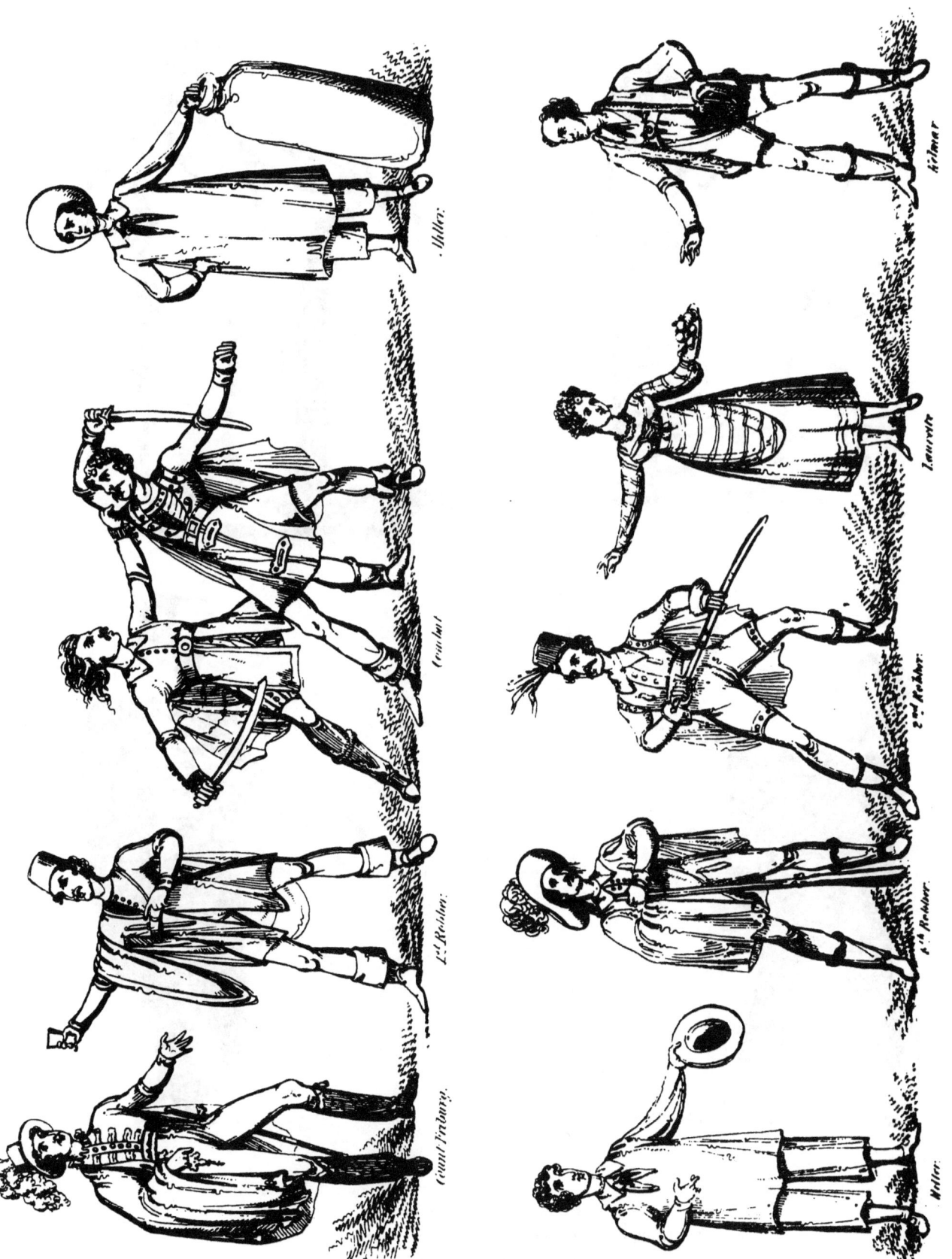

WEST'S CHARACTERS IN "THE MILLER AND HIS MEN"
Dated February 4, 1819.
From the British Museum Collection

AN EARLY EDITION
A Jameson sheet dated December 4, 1813.
From the British Museum Collection

But, supremest feature of all is that fiery, gory, and explosive end which is calculated to thrill all beholders.

Here undoubtedly we come upon the secret of the play's powerful appeal to the juvenile imagination.

The dialogue and construction of the play—at least in its various abridgements—have a naive charm which delights me whenever I read it. It opens with the good if sententious Kelmar uttering the phrase that Dickens loved: "Here's more grist to the mill."

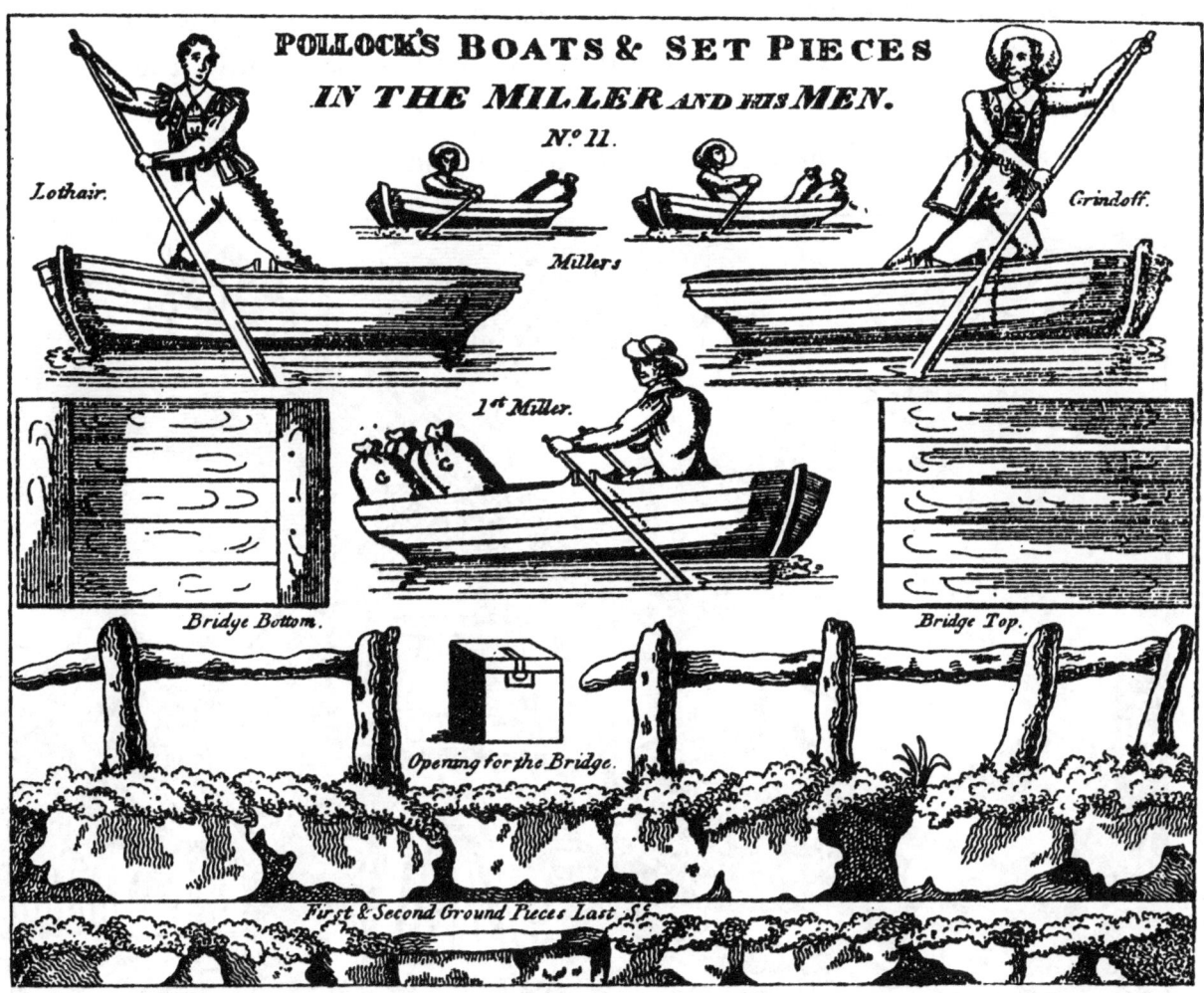

POLLOCK'S SET PIECES

Then he soliloquises thus: "This miller's fortune increases, for he was my tenant once and now I am a beggar compared with him. But never mind; although I am poor I am still respected for my honesty."

His daughter Claudine comes to talk to him about her love for Lothair. "Then father, dear father," she pleads. "Hear your Claudine! I never can consent to marry Grindoff; for this I know, the miller never can, with all his wealth make poor Claudine consent to love him."

That is according to the Hodgson version. In the Webb version Claudine, when the matter is broached says (with a sigh): "I fear I never can love the miller." Whereupon honest Kelmar says: "Then you never shall marry him. Think how poor Lothair is, but go in, child." "'Tis plain her heart is fixed on Lothair," he muses when she is gone, "and honest Grindoff yet must sue in vain."

Kelmar is unhappily rather mistaken about "honest Grindoff." He is, of course, a dissembler, and his real name is Wolf. His behaviour toward the unfortunate Claudine and the vengeful Ravina is horrible in the extreme and there are thrills in plenty until the grand explosion scene, when he and his companions are hurled to destruction.

The effect of that last scene 'comes over,' even on the printed page, and in spite of those bewildering and impossible stage directions which besprinkle the texts of the Juvenile Drama.

The scene is a 'close up' view of the mill which the robber crew use as a G.H.Q.

THE MILL IN PEACE (POLLOCK)

Grindoff, the disguised robber chief, appears, and so does Karl, who is on virtue's side. Then this dialogue ensues (I quote from the Webb version):

    GRIN. Ha ha! you strive in vain. I have sworn never to descend from this spot alive unless with liberty.
    KARL. Cowardly rascal! you shall have liberty to ascend from it. We'll send every rascal of you flying into the air on the sails of your own mill!

THE MILL EXPLOSION ACCORDING TO SKELT
From the British Museum Collection

And in spite of the awful threats and the bluff of Grindoff, Karl's dread prophecy is spectacularly fulfilled. The climax comes rapidly. I quote again:

> Enter LOTHAIR disguised in Golotz's cloak L.H. pl 5.
> GRIN. Quick! let my bride appear.
> Exit LOTHAIR L.H. Enter RAVINA with torch L.H. behind front ground piece.
> RAV. She is here! What would you?
> GRIN. Ravina! Traitress!
> RAV. Traitress! What then art thou? Ere it be too late make an atonement for thy many crimes.

Instead of offering to make atonement, however, the despicable but bold Grindoff continues to utter horrible threats, menacing the life of the virtuous Claudine in spite of the pitiful pleadings of her aged parent Kelmar.

Count Friberg, who is the feudal chief of these parts and owns his own army of grandly caparisoned warriors who all look exactly alike, threatens the robber chief with the arrival of reinforcements, whereat the undaunted Grindoff exclaims "For that threat be this my revenge."

He is apparently about to do something particularly awful and is, according to the stage directions "going off slowly L.H." when enter Lothair and Claudine "L.H. pl 7."

> LOT. And this Lothair's triumph.
> Retreats back L. GRINDOFF following, then put on GRINDOFF and LOTHAIR combating L.H. pl 7 GRINDOFF is wounded. Take off figures L.H.; put on GRINDOFF wounded pl 3, near to mill at back then enter LOTHAIR and CLAUDINE L.H. pl 7; the drawbridge is let down; they come over it or in front L.H.
> LOT. (to Ravina). Now Ravina fire the train.

And so Ravina does—or at least is supposed to do through the agency of the youthful stage director, and the effect is truly awful. In the words of Ravina who, woman-like, has the last word, "at one blow the hapless victims of captivity and insult are amply, dreadfully avenged." So the play comes to its fiery end.

"Loud explosions" are directed to be heard, the scene of the mill on peaceful inaction is rapidly withdrawn, disclosing the tableau which is the masterpiece of Webb's (or West's or Hodgson's, or Skelt's, or Pollock's) graphic art.

The mill is seen rent asunder by the gigantic explosion of the powder magazine. The air is filled with flame and smoke, pieces of timber and the mutilated bodies of the miserable members of the robber gang. In the foreground is the avenging Ravina complete with torch.

The stage directions add that most resplendent phrase—the clarion call to a frenzy of pyrotechnics—"Red fire to burn," and with the accompanying ignition "off," the banging of tin trays, the letting off of crackers and whatever other effects suggested themselves to the ingenuity of the juvenile producer the effect of this scene may be pronounced to be truly awful. The whole of the juvenile drama affords no spectacle so satisfying or approaching it for horror.

"No wonder" (as Brander Matthews comments) "that plate 7 and scene 11, No. 9, filled with joy the heart of Robert Louis Stevenson when he was a perfervid Scot of 14."

CHAPTER ELEVEN

THE BOOK OF THE PLAY

HIGH tribute has been paid to the quality of the drama of the miniature stage. The literary style of the plays varied considerably as, of course, it did in the originals, but in the main it must be admitted that those whose job it was to boil down the masterpieces of the current drama to the dimensions of the toy stage did their job surprisingly well. If sometimes authors condescended to reduce the volume of their own inspirations they were exceptions; many of the plays which were sold for a few pence were just hack work.

Besides recording the main characteristics of the action and the essential points of the dialogue they managed to extract that supreme essence—the 'Skeltery,' to use Stevenson's term—with considerable skill.

I have spent many a pleasant hour in browsing over these little books of the play. They are sometimes highly amusing because of their naive sentiments, their unconscious humour, their tawdry heroics, and their astonishingly ingenuous plots. It is difficult to believe that this kind of shoddy once occupied the attention and gained the plaudits of serious-minded and intelligent people. For remember that this sort of thing was the real stuff of the drama and not something specially invented for the amusement of juveniles.

Apart from the amusing qualities the miniature drama is worth serious study because here you get in a handy and condensed form an almost complete compendium of the dramatic output of an extensive period of the British stage.

I have made a selection of some of the most representative plays of the Juvenile Drama which covered a period of roughly fifty years. Many of them are plays that have become famous in the history of the British stage and some have even been performed within the memory of the middle-aged playgoer.

It is not always possible for me to name the exact source of the passage which I quote. Most of the better known plays—such as "Black-eyed Susan" and "Guy Fawkes"—appeared in different versions which vary considerably, and it is possible that much of the noble speeches, lofty sentiment, and picturesque rhodomontade is just as it appeared in the original script. In some cases I have gone to the Hodgson books of the play which in every way were excellently prepared; in others I have gleaned choice excerpts from the libraries of Webb and Pollock whose brevity and condensation and transcription were much more marked.

One of the most popular pieces of the Juvenile Drama repertory was "Black-eyed Susan," Douglas Jerrold's famous "nautical and domestic melodrama" (to use the official description) which was produced at the Surrey Theatre in 1824. It has been described as the best nautical melodrama ever written, and it certainly contains a number of fine scenes and stirring passages which, in spite of their high-flown sentiment, are still capable of exciting interest and of stirring the pulse.

Jerrold originally intended the piece for the Royal Coburg Theatre (now the "Old Vic") but quarrelling with Davidge the manager, he took it to Elliston of the Surrey Theatre, who engaged T. P. Cooke to play William, the leading part, at the then enormous salary of £60 a week. It is the role always to be associated with that notable actor and probably no one ever played it better.

The play was an immediate success and ran for a very long time, but although Elliston made thousands of pounds out of it, all that Jerrold received for it was the beggarly sum of £70. Of course a great deal of its popularity was due to the acting of Cooke, who was one of the best sailor heroes the British stage has ever known. Before turning to the stage at the age of eighteen Cooke had been a real sailor, and no one was his equal for making gallant, hearty speeches, dancing the hornpipe, wielding the cutlass, and doing whatever else the stage sailor had to do. He played the part of William in every theatre of Great Britain and continued to play it until he was over seventy years of age.

Cooke was a handsome, manly figure of a man and there is no more popular picture of him in the theatrical portrait gallery than that of Park's which depicts him in heroic attitude, his face fringed with black whiskers, a quaint little straw hat perched on his head, his right hand brandishing a cutlass and his left grasping—heaven knows to what purpose—a Union Jack.

"Black-eyed Susan" has an excellent plot. William, the sailor, arriving home suddenly finds a stranger attempting to kiss his wife and gallantly strikes at him with his ever-ready cutlass, believing him to be a buccaneer. He discovers to his horror that he has attacked his own captain.

So there is a court martial, for to strike a superior officer was an offence against the twenty-second Article of War, entailing the death penalty. Before the sentence is passed William makes a noble speech in defence of the right of a man to defend the honour of his wife. It is full of rich, nautical terms and the picturesque imagery of the seafaring man.

"I hadn't been gone the turning of an hour glass," he says, "when I heard Susan giving signals of distress. I out with my cutlass, made all sail and come up to my craft.

FIRST PLATE IN DYER'S "PIZARRO"
From the British Museum Collection

I found her battling with a pirate. I never looked at his figure-head, never stopped—would any of your honours? . . . You would have done as I did. And what did I? Why, I cut him down like a piece of old junk—had he been the First Lord of the Admiralty why, damme, I'd have done the same."

Then the death sentence is passed and there is a very affecting farewell scene between William and his Susan. Just then, however, in dashes Captain Crosstree with the glorious news that at the time of the offence William's discharge from the service had been granted, the document having been kept back " by villainy." So there has been no offence and William is freed amid loud huzzas.

Another favourite melodrama was " Jack Sheppard " which was produced at the Surrey Theatre in October 1839, glowingly described as " a new and singularly graphic melodrama and panoramic adaptation " by J. T. Haines. The play had been adapted from Harrison Ainsworth's novel against which there had been an outcry on the grounds that it was a glorification of the criminal. The outcry was renewed when the play was produced and in defence the playbill insisted that Ainsworth had been actuated by a high moral purpose " to show that there is no mortal, however wicked, without some redeeming virtue, that depravity, however covered by bravado is sure to entail punishment " and that " an ignominious death is the just reward of an atrocious life."

Nevertheless, in spite of these fine protestations, Jack Sheppard was really made the hero of romance. The real villain was Jonathan Wild who, having lured Jack into a life of crime betrayed him as he had done others.

The best version of the play was that produced by Buckstone at the Adelphi when Jack Sheppard was played by Mrs Keeley, Blueskin by Paul Bedford, and Jonathan Wild by O. Smith, the famous villain.

" Nix, my dolly pals, fake away," was one of the many popular lyrics introduced into the Buckstone version, which teems with thieves' slang now almost incomprehensible.

One of the great scenes in the play was the murder of Sir Rowland Trenchard, Jack's uncle and a horrible villain, by the equally horrible Jonathan Wild, the signal for which was the phrase " You have a long journey before you, Sir Rowland Trenchard."

While in the play as in the novel Jack Sheppard is depicted as a hero of romance the fact is that the real Jack, who was hanged at Tyburn in 1724 at the age of twenty, was a criminal of a rather commonplace kind. However, because of his youth and because his ingenious escape from Newgate appealed to the popular imagination he gained a sort of renown and thousands lined the route to Tyburn when he was hanged.

Some of the choicest twopence coloured rant appears in " Pizarro, or the Spaniards in Peru " which was produced on May 24, 1779 with Mrs Siddons, Kemble, and Barrymore in the cast. Yet this fustian stuff was by Sheridan, who was very proud of it. He had adapted it from the German play "The Death of Rolla" by Kotzebue and it is an odd fact that the last act was not completed until the very day of its production. Thus Edgar Wallace in slickness of output was long anticipated.

The adaptation was certainly very free. Sheridan knew no German. The translation was made by Marie Geisweiler, and Sheridan seems to have done what he liked with it. For instance one of the passages in the original ran:

> Thou whom neither the terror of the elements nor the fury of the foe were able to alarm.

This Sheridan turned into such elaborate bombast as:

> Thou, on Panaman's brow, didst make alliance with the warring elements, that tore the silence of the horrid night, when thou didst follow as the pioneer the crashing thunder's drift and stalking o'er the trembling earth didst plant thy banner at the red volcano's mouth.

This picturesque rant is equalled by the celebrated address of Rolla to the Peruvian soldiers. Sheridan was so proud of this showy stuff that he even incorporated it in his political addresses. Speaking of the craft of the bold invaders the patriotic Rolla says:

> They follow an adventurer whom they fear and obey a power which they hate; we serve a monarch whom we love—a god whom we adore. Whene'er they move in anger, desolation tracks their progress! Whene'er they pause in amity affliction mourns their friendship. They boast they come but to improve our state, enlarge our thoughts and free us from the yoke of error! Yes, they will give enlightened freedom in our minds who are themselves the slaves of passion, avarice, and pride. They offer us their protection; yes, such protection as vultures give to lambs—covering and devouring them.

And so on with a great deal more in the same high-flown vein.

The play has many picturesque and effective moments, however, including a fine scene in the Temple of the Sun where the Peruvian priests and priestesses chant their hymn to the sun. Nowadays I suppose people would laugh at such highly coloured stuff but the simpler-minded folk of its day hailed it with rapture. In the modern phrase "they ate it up" and as Elvira Mrs Siddons made one of her greatest successes.

"Pizarro" has not been seen since Samuel Phelps revived it at Sadlers Wells in 1866. Readers of Thackeray's *Pendennis* will remember that this was the play in which Miss Fotheringay appeared "looking uncommonly handsome in a white raiment and leopard skin, with a sun upon her breast and fine tawdry bracelets upon her beautiful, glancing arms."

"The Battle of Waterloo," one of Pollock's (or Green's) favourite pieces was, I suppose, one of the military and equine spectacles in which Astley's specialised. The title, of course, explains its scope, and Wellington, Napoleon, Blucher, and Marshal Ney are among its principal characters. Another character introduced is Molly Malony, an extra-

SCENE FROM "BLACK-EYED SUSAN"
Published by Dyer Senr. and Co.

ordinary woman who followed the 92nd Regiment from England and was found dead on the field of battle on June 18, 1815. Some of the speeches of Wellington and Napoleon, brief as they are, are worthy of note. There is, for instance, Napoleon's address to the outposts:

> Gentlemen: Your conduct as patriots and soldiers will, I doubt not, always obtain for you my approbation. With soldiers so resolute and generals so talented great results may be expected.

TITLE PAGE IN POLLOCK'S "THE BATTLE OF WATERLOO"

> Half Europe is arrayed against us. Good, be it so. I and my valiant Frenchmen know how to die but not to compromise the honour and safety of our beloved France. Onward! march!

Later on when Napoleon addresses a British prisoner he is good enough to observe that "English character may be calculated upon."

The way in which one victory follows another in this play is bewildering in its rapidity. A few words of dialogue and stage directions describing "immense fire" and "terrible cannonading" and another victory is won.

One cannot but admire the fine reticence and reserve with which Wellington announces the triumph of Waterloo. There is an animated scene, baldly indicated (and shorn of some of its technical bewilderments) by the stage directions:

> Enter Lord Hill and the British troops followed by the Duke of Brunswick and Brunswick Horse. R.—Enter Highlanders firing and English Artillery. Shells are thrown from each side of the stage. Screams, shrieks, and the double crack is heard.—Enter Life Guards L. cross the stage and exit R. Enter Molly Malony with pistols, rushed across the stage followed by a Highlander with a child on his back and a Lifeguardsman with French Eagle. Enter Napoleon followed by Cuirassiers and Life Guards fighting.—Enter the Duke of Wellington, Lord Hill, Gen. Blucher, British troops, Prussian soldiers.

Then says Wellington with soldierly brevity:

> "Gentlemen, the victory is decided in favour of the British Troops!"
> (Loud huzzas by the soldiery).

"Guy Fawkes, or the Gunpowder Treason," "a historical melodrama in three acts by George Macfarren" was produced at the Royal Coburg Theatre in 1820 when Guy Fawkes was played by O. Smith, the famous 'villain.' In the scene in the vault Guy Fawkes, preparing to blow Parliament sky high, has a magnificent soliloquy. There are many versions of it. I quote the following passage from Hodgson's book of the play:

"This situation most men would be afraid of [says Guy Fawkes administering comfort to himself in the dark vault] but I am not afraid to die. How many are there without whose feelings would paralyse them were they to hear one man lived who could thus willingly place himself upon the brink of death and look into the dark abyss with more than mortal pleasure!
(Distant sound of trumpets).
"Ha! the procession advances—the King and Queen, the court will soon be seated, their minds riveted alone to stately splendour will not anticipate so short a road to eternity; and as St Peter's clock strikes twelve the gaping crowd will view a scene of desolation and dream that Heaven sent an individual bold enough to punish tyranny and give a great and powerful people freedom."

However, of course, Guy Fawkes' unholy gloatings are interrupted by the entrance of Lord Montague crying "Monster, forbear!"

There is a terrific last scene in which, after the execution of Guy Fawkes, the conspirators perish in an explosion. The play ends, like "The Miller and his Men," with a tableau of the explosion and a grand display of fireworks and red fire.

"Alone in the Pirates' Lair," one of the many piratical dramas and the play which made its first appearance as a serial in *The Boys of England* is notable for this gem of dialogue which never failed to bring down the house:

Mark Ambrose (in deep sonorous tones, to Jack Rushton, a very young sailor hero whom he had persecuted and at whom he is now presenting a brace of pistols): "Back, boy, back! Dread thy doom! For English Jack is a name I hate!"
Jack (snapping his fingers at both pistols): "And fear too! my bold, black-hearted senor!"
(Crash of music).

"Tom and Jerry, or Life in London," very popular in its time as a sort of revue of Metropolitan fast life, opens at Hawthorn Hall (to the tune of "Willie brew'd a peck o' maut") with:

> Here we are met, all social boys
> That can enjoy a country spree;
> Friends of fox-hunting, fun and noise,
> So toss your bumpers off with glee.

It will be conceded that the verse is at least as good as the sentiment.

Tom tells the company that as Jerry will in all probability be adopted as a member of

MARKS'S *New Characters in* LIFE IN LONDON.
In 9 Plates.

Watchman

African Sal

Dusty Bob

Racket Master

Master of the Whistling Shop

The Gas Light Man

London. Published by J.L. Marks, 23, Russell Court Drury Lane

AN EXAMPLE OF J. L. MARKS'S WORK
From the British Museum Collection

Parliament for the borough of Hawthorn and have to reside in town he must soon be initiated into the life of London. "I have had some experience myself," he says, "and will be his mentor; he shall see the good and the bad, the high and the low. A knowledge of every class will enable him to decide impartially in the senate and by viewing the horrors of vice teach him the sterling value of virtue."

No one could take exception to these high sentiments and fine pretentions but alas! it would seem that this is only an elaborate excuse for doing a round of the more reprehensible sights of London. The young men are followed in their senatorial investigations by their ladies, Jane and Sue, who hit upon the novel idea of disguising themselves in men's clothes.

The heroes first visit Tattersall's and Almack's where they join in the singing of the chorus:

> Life in London how we feel,
> All our heads are on the reel,
> All our senses on the wing,
> Rapture strikes the trembling string.

Their further researches take them to Cribb's parlour, "a fashionable night hell in St James's" and "the back slums of Holy Land" where one of the girls disguises herself as Ballad Bet, the Clare Market Beauty. Here there is a "grand recognition." And having enjoyed himself at all these wild pleasures Tom has the solemn effrontery to bring down the curtain with this remarkable speech:

> "My wild oats are sown and not a seed left. We have seen life in London as it really is and shall derive profit and instruction from it all our lives. A correct knowledge of human nature such as we have attained, confers upon us two very important benefits—it increases the energy of virtue and diminishes the excesses of vice."

Pecksniff could not have bettered these sentiments.

There is some similarity to this play in "Life in Paris," a drama in three acts which must have been quite an amusing affair. The personages include Sir Humphrey Halibut, "knight, alderman, and fishmonger," Mumps, his son, Dick Wildfire, his nephew, and Ben Binnacle, a sailor, who is their man.

The whole party goes to Paris to see the sights and one and all behave like clowns and hooligans.

The various scenes give glimpses of the show places of Paris, including the Square du Chatelet "with its superb Fountain and Column," the Boulevard des Italiens by night, "the Resort of all Loungers of Paris with various exhibitions such as Rope-dancers, Tumblers, Punch, etc., and a whole Tribe of Flower Girls, Musicians, and Promenaders."

On reaching this delectable spot the whole party joins in the chorus:

> Oh this is the scene of Parisian delight
> Where beaming eyes of pleasure glancing,
> Laughing, jigging, good wine swigging,
> Fills up life's gay measure.

Later the English trippers visit a French theatre where the representation of French soldiers beating three Englishmen rouses the patriotic ire of Ben Binnacle who exclaims "No, no, that will never do; I can't stand by and be laughed at in that way; so here goes."

Then, according to stage directions, "Ben rushes up to the Stage, a general fight commences and the Scene ends with a jolly Row and Battle Royal."

The English visitors generally seem to have behaved in an highly objectionable way while in Paris but all ends happily, the last scene depicting the Gardens of the Tivoli illuminated and the assembly singing:

> Drive ev'ry care away,
> Kill sorrow, banish pain,
> Be merry here, I say
> Let life in Paris reign.

"The Infernal Secret, or the Invulnerable" must have been a gorgeously thrilling drama of the supernatural. When the play opens one sees the beautiful Isidora hotly beset by a wretch named Montilla.

Says this naturally alarmed girl: "I cannot describe the awe I feel when I behold this mysterious man. My whole frame trembles and my heart beats with agony even when he most exerts himself to gain my good opinion."

To which speech the mysterious Montilla replies: "Lady! when I behold such transcendant beauty is it possible not to feel a tender passion? Is it possible to behold the lovely Isidora and not express the sentiments of respect and admiration?"

This pretty speech, however, merely disguises the evil plans of Montilla, who is the "mysterious Being who knows no fear." In other words he is a creature doomed to live in instalments of 300 years provided at the end of each term he can marry "an untainted Catholic." Should he fail his existence is at an end.

The lovely Isidora suits his requirements but as she is an unwilling bride he obtains the help of the banditti. In spite of terrorism, however, he does not gain her and the drama ends frightfully.

"Montilla is almost distracted," runs the stage directions, "as the clock strikes twelve" and he sinks into a body of flames. The robbers are subdued, their cavern blows up and all ends happily for the persecuted Isidora.

"The Blood Red Knight, or the Fatal Bridge" is another strong melodrama rich in gore and deeds of darkness. It opens with a scene "in a wild country" and Isabella in

flight leading with her a child who exclaims: "Don't grieve, mother; my father will soon return and, remember, I shall grow up a man by and by and then I can protect you." The stage che-ild was ever thus.

Subsequently mother and child are delivered into the hands of the Blood-red Knight who carries on in a manner befitting his sinister title. On one desperate occasion he cries: "Remorse! I feel revenge! and since that brat is made an obstacle to my desires—thus—thus he shall perish."

He attempts to stab the unfortunate child but is prevented and, I am glad to say, disaster overtakes him in the end. He is killed and his entire band subjugated.

"The Exile, or the Coronation of Elizabeth" is a drama of the mountains of Siberia and the city of Moscow and the unfortunate hero is the much persecuted Count Ulrick whom one first encounters in exile. "Can it be possible," he exclaims with a pathos that must have rent many bosoms, "that my enemies are not yet satisfied? Robbed of property, of freedom, of strength, am I still to live in persecution and my exile prove the target for Enemy's darts—an object fixed upon as the sport of Malice?" The reflection may be taken as very nicely put in the circumstances.

His daughter Alexena goes to Moscow to plead for her father and arriving "exhausted from her journey" cries: "Where—where can I find to turn me for protection? No father, no mother, no friend to assist me, and if I should perish my poor exiled father will never be more restored to liberty! Ha! there is a house! I cannot bear up longer! Therefore I'll knock at yonder door and if the occupier has but common humanity he will not drive a famishing being from it."

Alexena, one learns with relief, falls among friends. There is a gorgeous procession in the square of Moscow consisting of soldiers, priests, bishops, Chinese troops, Knights of Malta, ambassadors, down to the lesser but equally picturesque fry. Alexena obtrudes upon this spectacle, presents a petition to the Empress and saves her father.

Someone has described "The Woodman's Hut, or the Burning Forest" as a very silly play. It is, though not more silly than a large number of melodramas which our forefathers dearly loved. It is a ridiculous story about counts and pursued maidens but it ends with that sovereign remedy for all weak plots—a fire, which rejoiced the adult playgoer as much as it gratified the juvenile theatre owner.

The heroine of this stirring drama indulges in some delicious soliloquies. Like many forlorn maidens in dire adversity she refers to herself constantly in the third person. Discovered in the interior of a humble cottage she muses:

> "How dreadfully the storm rages, the mountain torrents swelling the river give it a fearful violence—how long beneath this wretched hut must I, miserable Amelia, take shelter from her enemies."

But her speeches are not so good as those of Count Conenberg, the hero, who delivers himself of several addresses of careful phrasing and admirable formality. Hear his reply to his friend Werther when he remarks: "You have a splendid estate, why wear such a sad and melancholy face?"

"The tale is somewhat romantic, listen. In one of those excursions I frequently indulged in after the death of my father to enjoy the pleasure of solitude, overcome by my feelings I gave my horse the reins and seated myself upon a bank overlooking the river and while enjoying the beauty of the surrounding scenery my reverie was broken by the shrieks of a female apparently in distress; I arose and hastened to the spot from whence the cries proceeded and there beheld a female of such exquisite beauty that has left an impression on my heart never to be erased."

"Proceed, the tale is highly romantic," says the appreciative Werther.

So the Count goes on with his tale until a servant enters whereupon he breaks off remarking in a business-like fashion: "If I mistake not this is a mission from Baron Hernhausen, the enemy of our house; excuse me, my friend, for even the theme of love must yield to the stern diction of honour."

The Count discourses in like manner all the way through the play, which ends in good, incendiary style, for the last scene discloses cottage and wood "in a blaize," according to stage directions.

There remain the pantomimes, in which the Juvenile Drama was very rich. A study of these is instructive as well as amusing—instructive because they are of a type of entertainment that has almost passed away. With them has gone that aroma of oranges and gaslight than which old stagers will declare there never was richer incense. If you wish to know the type of pantomime in which the great Grimaldi excelled you will find it illustrated here. Here are enshrined puns of an excruciating kind, quaint rhymed couplets and topical references of which the significance and application have long been lost.

For instance in "Whittington and his Cat, or Harlequin Lord Mayor of London"—a "new grand old English pantomime" Miss-Fortune addressing Miss-Chief in "The Miss-managed abode of Miss-Fortune" says:

> You're always ready *my alarum* to bring,
> No miss e'er yet objected to a ring.

Later on Miss-Fortune says:

> Our friend John Bull has given over grumbling,
> And e'er the farmers spurning my restraints
> Are making money where they make complaints;
> To talk about misfortune now's a folly
> Where everybody's bent on being jolly.
> Miss-Chance: The Crystal Palace you attacked in vain.
> Miss-Fortune: You've gone and built a better one again.
> Miss-Chance: Ah, even Ireland is improved and drained.

ONE OF POLLOCK'S PANTOMIMES

And there were puns of this sort:

> I'm tired of this stormy occupation
> And want a little wreckreation.

Dick Whittington on Highgate Hill delivers himself thus:

> I'm tired already 'tis a wild goose chase,
> I'll try a small investment on this bank,
> I've nothing else to save through Fortune's malice
> And so I'll save my breath and dream of Alice.

You will find obscure topical references which no doubt in their time made the public roar with appreciation in "Harlequin Baron Munchausen."

> 2nd Imp: Any humbug pockets John Bull's money.
> Mischief: Ah, true, with bills and puffs each his trade
>   will urge on.
> 1st Imp: Moses—
> 2nd Imp: Cheap bedding—
> 3rd Imp: Artful dodgers—
> 4th Imp: Spurgeon.
> Mischief: It's all excitement, there a general fuss is,
>   The fever even has attacked the buses;
>   If a saloon you hail and try to rush in
>   You can't.
> 2nd Imp: And, why?
> Mischief: It's out a-nursing.

Or the Queen complained:

> This is an age of improvement,
>   Nothing need be thought romantic.
> The British Queens spoke to the President
>   Through the Atlantic.

The Harlequinade part of all these pantomimes yields but little in the way of dialogue. A study of scenes will give you an idea of the business in which clown, pantaloon, harlequin, and columbine engaged. It consisted mainly of horseplay, cruel practical jokes upon guileless folk, and many trick changes of scene. As a matter of fact, I believe, the dialogue was never committed to print. The business may have existed in manuscript form some time or other, but it is more probable that all the traditional dialogue was just handed down by word of mouth. Such as there is in the little pages of the Juvenile Drama conveys only a shadow of the fun and spirit of the Harlequinade of the glorious past.

CHAPTER TWELVE

TINSEL PORTRAITS

Although, strictly speaking tinsel pictures do not form part of the cult of the toy theatre they are so closely allied to the business that the subject can hardly be ignored in a book of this character. All the great masters of the toy theatre like West, Park, Lloyd, Skelt, and Webb were equally notable for their theatrical portraits, and there were others like Fairburn who more particularly specialised in them.

Tinsel pictures were an elaboration of the theatrical prints which, a hundred years or so ago before the era of the picture postcard and the illustrated Press, were sold by thousands.

No theatrical history of the nineteenth century can be considered complete without a study of these theatrical portraits and their tinselled elaborations which showed stage favourites of the day in their principal roles. Nearly all the famous actors and actresses of the early half of the last century figured in these portraits, and the hobby of tinselling them must have given hours of pleasure to hundreds of lovers of the theatre and admirers of popular stage artists.

In those days you bought a picture of your favourite actor for a few pence and proceeded to spend anything up to a pound or so in decorating it with tinsel 'dots,' armour, warlike accoutrements, little bits of satin and silk, etc., until the complete thing became very grand indeed and positively dazzling to look upon. The finished picture was generally framed in a heavy frame of maple wood. Then came a time when these parlour ornaments were looked down upon as evidence of early Victorian bad taste and vulgarity, and they were relegated to the lumber-room, the garret, and the second-hand shop.

The vogue of chromo-lithography and the taste for pretty-pretty pictures of highly sentimental subjects in the fifties and sixties of the last century put the tinsel pictures into disfavour. Hundreds of them for which to-day many collectors would be willing to pay much money were cast aside in favour of their worthless successors. There has since been a revival in favour of these quaint old pictures, however, and if you can pick up a good specimen in its original frame of black or of maple wood for twenty shillings or so you may consider yourself lucky. But you must beware of the bogus tinsel picture. The demand is such nowadays that the false tinsel picture has been manufactured.

The experienced eye can easily detect the fake from the real. The real is to be detected by the quality of the paper on which it is mounted, the date marked on the picture, the

THEATRICAL PRINT ENGRAVED BY R. CRUIKSHANK AND COLOURED BY H. J. WEBB

character and style of the subject, and the marks of age on the print. It is true that some of the best specimens of tinsel pictures are entirely without such marks of age for the simple reason that they have been preserved in books and portfolios and not exposed to the influence of light.

There are many collections of tinsel pictures to-day the value of which probably runs into hundreds of pounds. The late Harry Furniss, the artist, had one of the finest collections ever got together in this country.

There is a quaint decorative charm about the tinsel picture at its best that accounts for the revulsion of taste in its favour. The heroic attitudes of the subjects—always depicted with one knee bent, with arms extended and with fierce grim countenance and a dwarfed perspective of country or camp as a background—are elements in a composition that unites humour, sentiment, stage history, and pictorial interest.

The tinsel picture seems to have come into vogue about 1830. Before that time the theatrical publishers had issued prints of actors and actresses in their favourite roles and in those pre-picture postcard days they had a popular sale. Then someone had a bright idea of ornamenting the pictures with little bits of metallic paper. The fad soon became popular and all the theatrical print dealers adopted the idea, though Webb took the lead, his uncle, a gunsmith, being, as we have seen, the first to make steel punches for stamping out the tinsel ornaments. At first tinsel ornamentation such as scale armour had each scale stamped out separately, but later the die was made in one piece, and it does not take an expert to detect the difference.

The tinsel was composed of copper foil in different colours with a paper backing. The art of making foil and paper adhere apparently died out with Mr W. G. Webb. For many years it has been impossible to obtain these tinsel ornaments. A whole armoury of dies required for the purpose lies rusty and dusty in Mr H. J. Webb's little shop. Many have disappeared, but the vast quantity remaining will give some idea of the extent and variety of the tinsel ornaments once obtainable. There were stock ornaments as well as the special sort required as each new part was issued.

For all the multitude of different ornaments a different die was used, each particular portrait requiring its own little pieces of decoration.

The subject of the picture was nearly always a leading actor or actress caught in a noble, bellicose, or menacing attitude. Pirates, brigands, monarchs, and warriors were the favourite subjects because the picturesqueness and brightness of the costumes lent themselves to dazzling and profuse ornamentation. T. P. Cooke in his many heroic roles, Farley (a famous Grindoff), Edmund Kean, Hicks, Macready, Payne, O. Smith, Liston, and Mrs Siddons were popular subjects, and Harlequins were a good selling line because they were spangled all over.

Of the bedazzlement offered by the choicest specimens of the tinselled portrait Albert

Smith, among other Victorian novelists, frequently wrote. If you have read *Christopher Tadpole* you may perhaps remember how Sprouts, after he had become the proud proprietor of the little stationer's and newsagent's shop in Lambeth, found business flourishing and an increased demand for theatrical portraits " which last had led him to add to his store a collection of gorgeous tinsel dots and stars and lions to adorn the different heroes. And as a specimen of their effect he had Mr Hicks, as 'The Avenger,' in a panoply so dazzling that no eye might have borne him in the sun."

In the same novel, which was written in 1844 (about which time the portraits were at the height of their vogue), he makes reference to " the theatrical portraits of heroes in very determined attitudes. Mr Huntley as El Hyder was violently opposed to Mr Macready as William Tell, and there was a horse combat between Kerim and Sanballat of a fierceness that threatened to annihilate everything."

One may get a hint as to the style of acting once so admired from a study of these prints. It is not mere caprice or convention that led the artist always to depict his subject in striking and noble attitude and with legs and arms always extended. With rant and florid heroics of speech went violent action. An actor of the calm and repose of the modern school of realism would have had few admirers in the good old days of the Coburg and Surrey melodrama.

A complete collection of tinsel pictures would probably include representations of every tragedian and tragedienne who was known during the first half of the last century. Macready as Macbeth and Kemble as the Merry Monarch were two of the most popular subjects; the latter because of his elaborate finery which lent itself admirably to the art of the tinseller. However popular were the Hamlets of the time, they were a poor selling line because of the drabness of their sable costumes.

Curiously enough actresses were not so popular among the public, but there was sufficient reason for this. For one thing, women's dress, in spite of its frills and flounces and fal-lals, did not lend itself half so well to tinsel decoration as that of the men who disported themselves in all the brave panoply of armour and in all the picturesque etceteras associated with the profession of soldier, bandit, and pirate.

But the chief reason was probably the fact that the artists who limned the pictures were never particularly successful in capturing the loveliness of their female subjects. No admirer of any of the famous stage beauties of the time would have thought of purchasing any of the portraits to remind him of the loveliness of the original. There was a uniform ugliness and hardness of feature over all the portraits no matter whom they represented. The Regency dresses in which they were invariably depicted gave them a dowdy, prim, and forbidding look. There must have been beauties who stirred the hearts of men with their perfection of form and feature in the old days just as they do now, yet one would not gather so after surveying the whole gallery of tinsel portraits. The

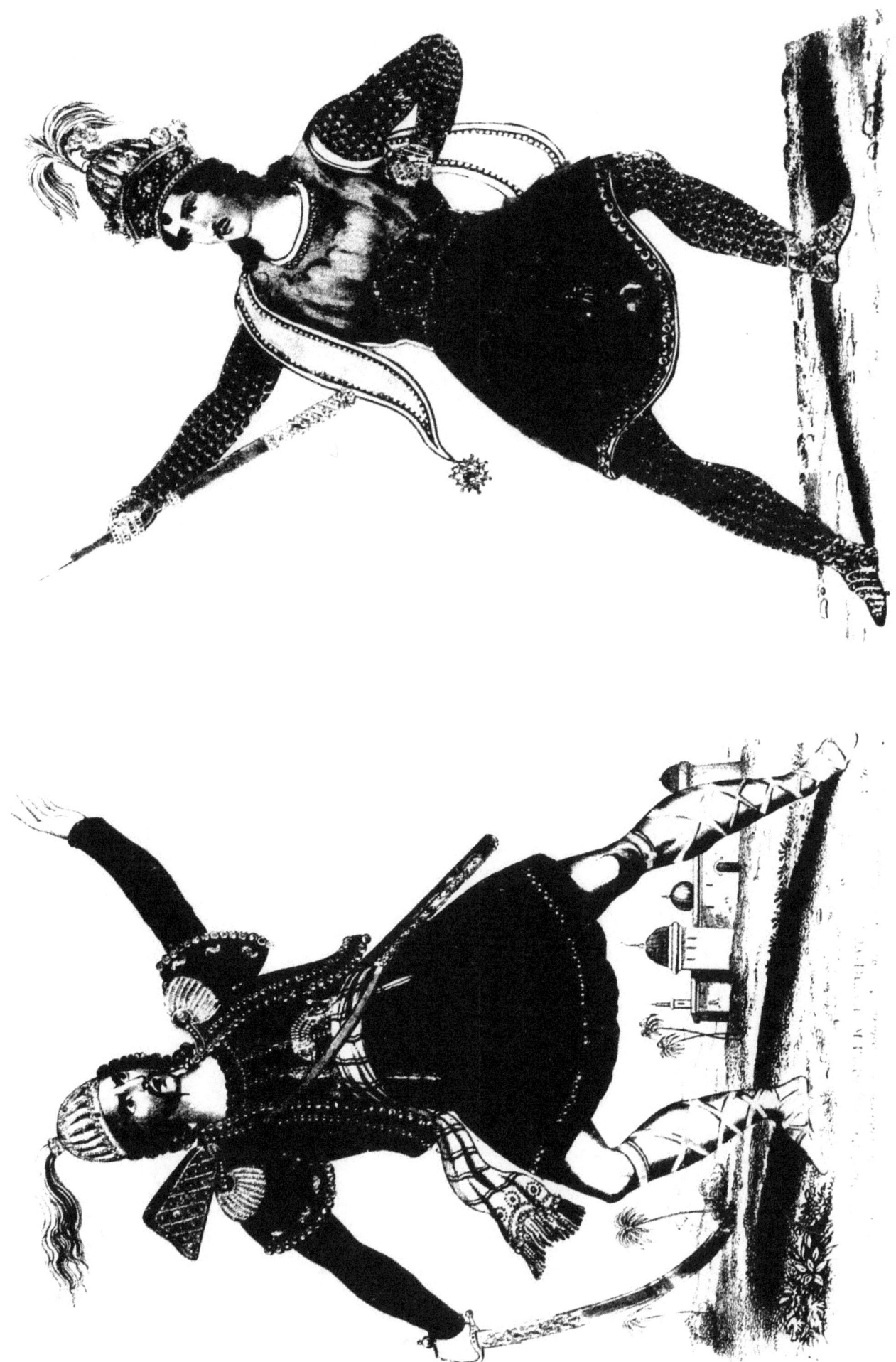

A PAIR OF PARK'S TINSELLED PORTRAITS
From the British Museum Collection

insipidity and uniformity of feature among these ladies grieves the heart and affronts the eye and makes us wonder what standard of beauty our forbears possessed. This inability of all the artists to transfer feminine loveliness on to the copper plate is a singular defect and characteristic of the tinsel portraits, particularly as the artists were very successful in capturing the likenesses of their male subjects.

Among the actresses who did figure prominently in the tinsel picture gallery were Mrs Faucit as the Queen of Denmark and the Empress Elizabeth, Fanny Kemble as Juliet (but what a Juliet!), Mme. Vestris in many of her famous roles, Louisa Pyne, Miss M. Woolf, and Miss E. Daly.

In the last year of his life Mr W. G. Webb, who probably knew more about the tinsel picture trade than any man, gave a peculiar reason for the decline in accuracy of portraiture which overtook the art. He said it was because of the rage for tinselling. Ultimately most of the efforts of the artists and engravers were devoted to putting buttons and epaulettes, shields and gauntlets, helmets and swords, and gilded sandals and belts into the pictures. The pictures became less and less like portraits.

"Why," he said, "the manner in which some of these pictures were decorated was little short of marvellous. Take the picture of Kean as Richard III; it is one of Johnson's of St Martin's Lane—one of the Skelt plates. Well, it would be painted and then possibly a little piece of gold or silver would be stuck on it. Then the trunks, cloak, sleeve, and tights would be covered with tiny strips of satin or silk in the proper colour, the feather would be covered with a real feather and the boots with bits of leather. Think of the time and patience for such work!"

The tinselling of pictures was a hobby on which one could lavish quite a lot of money. The extent to which the craze took hold of the public may be gauged somewhat by examining the dies from which Mr Webb and his employees once upon a time stamped out the little patterns. Some of these long, chisel-shaped pieces of steel originally measuring from six to ten inches in length were reduced to two or three inches by continual use. The outpot of 'dots' must have been enormous.

The tinselling of portraits while it engrossed the elders was also a pastime of youth. It was even introduced as a subject of art work in schools and now and again you may come across a picture with the marks awarded by the master to the pupil. Who shall say that this agreeable task did not help to encourage the taste for form and colour in the youthful mind as well as to inculcate a taste for the theatre?

The young tinsellers could exercise their skill not only upon stage subjects, for apart from theatrical celebrities Royalty occasionally figured in the portrait gallery. The accession of Queen Victoria and her marriage to the Prince Consort gave to the publishers two popular subjects. The Royal Pair in the Coronation robes made figures of a splendour sufficient to rival the most popular of brigands and Harlequins. Queen

Adelaide was also to be obtained. Military heroes, too, were sometimes to be encountered. Wellington and Napoleon were highly popular subjects.

In addition to the large-size character portraits the publishers issued many smaller pictures. Some of them were engraved four on a sheet and were popularly known as 'fours.' As many as six and eight different figures were sometimes engraved on one sheet.

As an admirer of the tinselled art I would most strongly urge that these pictures which have often been relegated to the lumber room are by no means to be disregarded. They have a quaint and picturesque decorative quality which is entirely their own. They are more decorative and pleasing to the eye than other Victorian fancies which have returned to favour. They form, at least as far as the male characters are concerned, the only contemporary portraits available of many interesting and eminent artists depicted in the actual costumes worn in their most popular roles.

From another point of view these quaint relics of a Victorian fad are by no means to be despised. The genuine tinselled portrait becomes scarcer every year. A really good specimen, if you can pick it up cheaply, may be regarded as a good investment likely to increase in value as time goes on.

APPENDIX A

PUBLISHERS

The following is, as far as I have been able to ascertain, a complete list of publishers of toy-theatre prints. The probable years in which they began business—where I have been able to obtain the information—is shown in parentheses:

Andrews and Co.	St Luke's.
J. Bailey (1830)	2 Slade's Place, Little Sutton Street; 66 Gray's Inn Lane; 188 Fleet Street; 3 Clifford's Inn.

(Probably he was only a printer to the trade)

G. Bishop and Co.	Houndsditch.
E. J. Brett and Co. (1866)	Publishers of *Boys of England*, Fleet Street.
T. W. Brown	10 May's Buildings, St Martin's Lane.
H. Burtenshaw (1812)	130 St Martin's Lane.
Carr	Houndsditch.
T. Christoe (1819)	34 Drury Lane.
W. Clarke (1821)	265 High Holborn.
W. Cole (1828)	10 Newgate Street.

(He took over some of Hodgson's publications and Park is said to have drawn for him)

G. Creed (1819)	Exeter Street, Strand.
D'Ash (1826)	27 Fetter Lane.
Dighton (1812)	
J. Dyer and Dyer and Co. (1828)	13 Dorset Crescent, Hoxton New Town; 109 Aldersgate Street.
Dyer, Jun.	33 (later 53) Bath Street, City Road.
F. Edwards (1828)	49 Leman Street, Goodman's Fields.
J. Fairburn (1837)	106 Minories.
J. Goodman (?1812)	Pentonville.
J. K. Green (?1808)	33 Salisbury Place, Walworth New Town; 3 George Street, Walworth New Town; 34 Lambeth Square, New Cut; 9 Thurlow Place, East Street, Walworth, etc.
W. Hawley	5 Seymour Road, Euston Square.
M. Hibberd (Mrs) (?1811)	2 Upper Carlton Street, Marylebone.
Hodgson and Co (1811)	11 Cloth Fair; 10 Newgate Street.
O. Hodgson (1811)	132 Fleet Street.
C. Hook (1820)	35 Windmill Street, Tottenham Court Road.
H. J. Jameson (1811)	13 Duke Street, Bow Street.
W. B. Johnson	St Martin's Lane.
H. Kenilworth	43 King Street, Snow Hill.

W. T. Layton (1820)	10 Petty's Court, Oxford Street.
R. Lloyd	40 Gibson Street.
W. Love (?1837)	81 Bunhill Row.
J. L. Marks (1839)	17 Artillery Street, Bishopsgate; 91 Long Lane, Smithfield; 23 Russell Court, Drury Lane.
H. Masters (1822)	Leigh Street, Red Lion Square.
H. Matthews (1887)	Churchfield Road, Acton.
W. Park	47 Leonard Street, Finsbury.
B. Perkins	40 Carnaby Market.
B. Pollock (1877)	73 Hoxton Street.

(He succeeded Redington in business)

J. Quick	4 Duke's Court, Union Street, Blackfriars Road.
J. Redington (1838)	208 Hoxton Old Town (later 73 Hoxton Street).
Shorman	Great Poulteney Street.
M.; M. & B.; E. Skelt (1830)	11 Swan Street, Minories.
J. Smart (1823)	35 Rathbone Place, Oxford Street.
W. Smith	
J. Spencer (1815)	63 East Street, Manchester Square.
S. Stokes (Mrs) (1832)	57 Wych Street.

(She was the successor to West's business)

D. Straker	21 Aldersgate Street.
W. G. Webb (1838)	Ripley, Surrey; Cloth Fair; Bermondsey Street; 49 (later 146) Old Street, St Luke's.
H. J. Webb (1890)	146 (later 124) Old Street.

(He succeeded to his father's business)

J. T. Wood	278 Strand.
W. West (1811)	Exeter House, Exeter Street, Strand; 57 Wych Street.

APPENDIX B

WEST'S PLAYS

Following is a list of West's plays with the date of their publication and the names of the theatres at which those plays reproduced were originally performed:

1811

February 26	The Peasant Boy	
July 2	Dulce Domum	Sadler's Wells
,, 30	The Council of Ten, or the Lake of the Grotto	Sadler's Wells
,, 31	Macbeth	Covent Garden
August 5	Lady of the Lake	Surrey
September 11	Tyrant and Saracen, or the Noble Moor	Astley's
October 9	Raymond and Agnes	Covent Garden
,, 29	The Iron Chest	
November 9	Don Juan	Royalty

1812

January 8	The Golden Fish	Covent Garden
March 5	Baghvan Ho!	Astley's
April 5	Julius Cæsar	
,, 17	Old Beelzebub, or Harlequin in Holland	Astley's
May 6	The Secret Mine	Covent Garden
,, 10	Valentine and Orson	Surrey
July 4	Harlequin Colossus	Surrey
August 1	Harlequin Jack and Jill, or the Clown's Disasters	Lyceum
October 5	Spanish Patriots	
November 4	Hag of the Lake	

1813

April 21	Ferdinand of Spain, or Ancient Chivalry	Astley's
June 20	Llewellyn Prince of Wales	
September 23	The Blood-red Knight, or the Fatal Bridge	
October 31	Manfredi	

1814

January 19	Harlequin Harper	Drury Lane
November 7	Illusion	

1815

March 12	Knight of the Black Plume	
April 25	Wallace the Hero of Scotland	
May 21	Comus, a Masque	
,, 24	Merry Wives of Windsor	
July 20	Harlequin Brilliant, or the Clown's Capers	
,, 20	Welsh Chieftains	

1815
October 27 — Romeo and Juliet
December 11 — Cymon

1816
February 7 — Harlequin and Fancy — Drury Lane
March 4 — The Broken Sword — Covent Garden

1817
July 1 — The Libertine
,, 22 — Richard III
,, 22 — Jack Sprat and his Cat

1818
January 28 — Harlequin and Red Dwarf — Covent Garden
August 15 — Falls of the Clyde
November 17 — El Hyder — Coburg

1819
February 4 — The Miller and his Men — Covent Garden
April 7 — The Forty Thieves
,, 16 — Pope Joan (pantomime) — Coburg
May 1 — Jack the Giant-killer — Regency
,, 11 — Hamlet
July 9 — The Blind Boy — English Opera
September 3 — Robert the Bruce, or the Battle of Bannockburn
December 11 — Beauty and the Beast — Coburg

1820
January 14 — Dervise of Bagdad, or Harlequin of Persia — Regency
October 20 — The Vampire — English Opera House
December 1 — The Abbot, or Mary Queen of Scots — Theatre of Varieties

1821
January — — The Coronation (a facsimile of the coronation of George IV) — Drury Lane
,, — The Exile — Covent Garden
March 14 — The Temple of Death — Coburg
April 10 — Rob Roy

1822
January 22 — Cherry and Fair Star
February 4 — Tom and Jerry — Adelphi

1823
December — — Conquest of Mexico — Covent Garden

1824
January 1 — Harlequin and Hero — Drury Lane
,, 24 — Harlequin and the Swans — Covent Garden
February 3 — Horatii and Curiatii
March 23 — Montrose
March 29 — The Dog of Montargis
,, 29 — Lodonais
,, 29 — The Death of Christophe, King of Hayti — Coburg
April 15 — Black Beard
,, 23 — Tom Thumb
,, 29 — Ivanhoe

1824

April 29	Rob Roy	
,, 30	The Red Witch	
May 8	The Battle of Waterloo	Davis's Amphitheatre
,, 30	Korastikan Prince of Assassins	
June 4	Bertram	
,, 14	The Battle of the Bridges	
,, 14	The Tiger's Horde	
July 5	Blue Beard	Covent Garden
August 8	High-mettled Racer	Astley's
,, 19	Henry IV	
,, 21	Lodoiska	Surrey
September 21	Philip Quarl, or the English Hermit	Coburg
October 8	Edward the Black Prince	Coburg
,, 13	Brigand and the Maid	
,, 25	La Perouse, or the Desert Island	English Opera House

1825

January 3	The White Cat, or Harlequin in the Fairy Wood	Covent Garden
,, 7	Harlequin Whittington, or Lord Mayor of London	Covent Garden
April 16	Guy Mannering	
May 8	Invasion of Russia	Royal Amphitheatre
,, 11	The Brave Cossack, or the Secret Enemy	Astley's
July 3	The Little Hunchback	
,, —	Telemachus	
,, —	The Mandarin, or Harlequin in China	Astley's
,, 29	Aladdin, or the Wonderful Lamp	

1826

February 1	The Casket of Gloriana	Regency
March 10	Malvina	Drury Lane
October 11	Paul Pry	Royal Amphitheatre

1827

March 15	The Wild Boy of Bohemia	Olympic
August 1	Timour the Tartar	Covent Garden
September 1	The Old Oak Chest	
December 12	Casco Bay, or the Mutineer	

1828

April —	The Pilot, or Storm at Sea	Adelphi
November 2	The Bottle Imp	

1829

March 19	Red Rover	
September 8	Black-eyed Susan	Surrey
December —	The Elephant of Siam, or the Fire Fiend	Adelphi

1830
Nothing appears to have been published

1831

February 2	Olympic Revels	Olympic
,, 9	The Brigand	Drury Lane
—	Death of Zouchi	Minor Theatre, Catherine Street

BIBLIOGRAPHY

The most interesting articles upon the subject of the Juvenile Drama include:

"A Penny Plain and Twopence Coloured" in *Memories and Portraits* by
R. L. Stevenson

Savage Club Papers 1868	Article by	Edward Draper
The Era Almanac 1870	do do	John Oxenford
The Theatre 1886	do do	Godfrey Turner
The Art Journal 1887	do do	William Archer
The Era Almanac 1891	do do	Theo Arthur
Varia 1894	do do	John Ashton
The Dickensian March 1908	do do	Percy Fitzgerald
Evening News December 16, 1908	do on	"Toy Theatre Makers"
The Pall Mall Gazette December 4, 1910	do by	Ralph Middleton
The Daily Chronicle September 12, 1912	do do	S. R. Littlewood
The Mask April 1913	do do	Dr Francis Eagle
The Daily Chronicle January 7, 1914	do do	S. R. Littlewood
Scribner's Magazine October 1915	do do	Dr Brander Matthews
The London Journal (Spare Moments) January 29, 1921	do do	Frank Jay
The Drama (New York) April 1925	do do	Stanley Nott

INDEX

A. PEOPLE

Ainsworth, Harrison, 95
Andrews and Co., 60
Archer, William, 16, 23, 29, 37, 46, 49, 83
Arthur, Theo, 32, 39, 47, 55, 83
Ashton, John, 16, 23, 79

Bailey, 81
Bishop, 83
Blake, William, 42, 43, 46
Blanchard, E. L., 47
Blatchford, Robert, 26
Brett, E. J., 58, 59, 83
Burtenshaw, 30, 35

Chaplin, Charles, 69, 65
Chesterton, G. K., 26, 69
Childs, George, 44, 52
Churchill, Winston, 26, 69, 72
Clapp, John Bouvé, 27
Cole, 53
Cooke, T. P., 35, 46, 47, 94, 105
Cooper, Gladys, 69, 75
Cox, David, 35
Craig, Gordon, 26, 69, 75
Cruikshank, George, 15, 42, 43, 44, 45, 46, 48, 52, 53, 70
Cruikshank, Robert, 42

Diaghileff, 69
Dickens, Charles, 22, 26, 69, 71, 86, 87
Dighton, Robert, 42
Douglas, Capt. R. H., 43
Draper, Edward, 50
Dyer, 35, 53, 54, 55

Eagle, Dr F., 67
Enthoven, Mrs Gabrielle, 15

Fairburn, 51
Farley, 79, 83, 105
Finden, William, 42
Fitzball, Edward, 77
Fitzgerald, Percy, 86, 87
Flaxman, 42, 46
Frith, W. P., 26
Furniss, Harry, 67, 105

Goethe, 21
Green, J. K., 28 29, 30, 31, 32, 36, 41, 57, 96
Grimaldi, 46, 67, 81, 82
Gröber, Karl, 33, 34
Grundy, Sydney, 26

Hamilton, Walter, 64
Hawley, 59
Heath, 42, 70
Hibberd, Mrs, 35, 52
Hodgetts, Capt. F., 15
Hodgson, 14, 28, 31, 34, 35, 39, 51, 52, 54, 58, 65, 70, 71, 80

Irving, Sir Henry, 26

Jameson, H. J., 14, 34, 35, 53, 65
Jerrold, Douglas, 94

Kean, Edmund, 35, 40, 46, 105
Kemble, John, 40, 95

Lamb, Charles, 79
Lane, Lupino, 69, 73, 75
Lane, Mrs Sarah, 75
Levi, Langley, 63
Lillo, George, 85
Liston, 35, 46, 78, 83, 105
Lloyd, R., 29, 54, 104
Lyons, 85

[115]

Macready, 35, 105, 106
Marks, J. L., 57
Matthews, 60
Matthews, Dr Brander, 85, 92
Millais, Sir John Everett, 26
Munden, 35, 46, 78
Munster, Earl of, 72

Nott, Stanley, 50

O'Neill, Mrs, 40
Oxenford, John, 16, 20, 24, 26, 45

Park, 28, 53, 54, 55, 57, 64, 70, 104
Perkins, 59
Phelps, Samuel, 96
Pinero, Sir A., 68, 85
Pocock, Isaac, 83, 85
Pollock, B., 14, 16, 37, 39, 58, 62, 65, 69, 70, 72 73, 74, 96
Prior, E. P., 15, 30, 50

Quick, 59

Redington, 30, 35, 57, 58, 71, 76

Sheridan, 95, 96
Sherson, Errol, 78
Siddons, Mrs, 40, 95, 96, 105
Sims, G. R., 26

Sitwells, The, 69, 73
Skelt, 14, 15, 28, 29, 35, 36, 41, 50, 51, 54, 55, 56, 57, 58, 62, 65, 66, 70, 81, 83, 104
Smith, Albert, 50, 106
Smith, O., 46, 98, 105
Spencer, 35
Stevenson, Robert Louis, 14, 21, 29, 54, 55, 61, 62, 68, 69, 71, 73, 75
Stothard, 42
Stokes, Mrs, 50, 53

Terry, Edward, 26
Terry, Ellen, 26, 75
Thackeray, W. M., 45, 96
Thomas, Ralph, 14, 43, 44, 46, 48, 49, 56
Toole, J. L., 26
Tree, Beerbohm, 26
Turner, Godfrey, 16, 42, 44, 47

Vestris, Mme, 28, 40, 46, 107

Walden, Lord Howard de, 33
Webb, H. J., 14, 15, 56, 62, 63, 67, 70, 71, 105
Webb, W. G., 35, 39, 53, 56, 62, 64, 65, 67, 68, 69, 70, 87, 104, 105, 107
West, William, 14, 28, 29, 30, 31, 34, 35, 42, 43, 44, 45, 46, 47, 48, 49, 50, 54, 55, 58, 65, 70, 79, 82, 86, 104

Yeats, Jack B., 60

B. PLAYS

Abbot, The, 46
Aladdin, 31, 35, 55, 56, 64, 82
Ali Pacha, 52
Alone in the Pirates' Lair, 58, 98
Americans, The, 53
Avenger, The, 106

Baghvan Ho! 46
Battle of the Alma, 32, 36, 64, 68
Battle of Inkerman, 64
Battle of Waterloo, 31, 36, 68, 74, 96
Bertram, 43, 53
Black-eyed Susan, 31, 36, 46, 78, 80, 93, 94
Blood-red Knight, The, 36, 100
Blue Beard, 47, 55, 59

Bottle Imp, The, 78
Brigand's Son, The, 36
Broken Sword, The, 43

Captain Ross, 57
Casco Bay, 47, 80
Cataract of the Ganges, 80
Charles the Bold, 53
Charles the Second, 43, 57, 74
Cherry and Fair Star, 82, 86
Chevy Chase, 39
Comus, 53
Coriolanus, 47
Corsair, The, 53
Corsican Brothers, The, 73
Council of Ten, The, 29

Dame Crump, 68
Death of Rolla, The, 96
Der Freischütz, 55
Don Juan, 43, 53
Dred, or the Dismal Swamp, 68
Dulce Domum, 82

Elephant of Siam, 47
Esmeralda, 60
Exile, The, 43, 101

Fairy of the Oak, 35
Falls of the Clyde, 43
Flying Dutchman, The, 31, 43
Forest of Bondy, The, 31, 68
Forty Thieves, The, 31, 35, 36, 47, 49, 53, 55, 59

George Barnwell, 85
Giant Horse, The, 52
Giant of the Blue Mountains, The, 59
Golden Fish, The, 35, 82
Guy Fawkes, 15, 52, 93, 98
Guy Mannering, 43

Harlequin Baron Munchausen, 103
Harlequin and Blue Beard, 82
Harlequin Brilliant, or the Clown's Capers, 43
Harlequin and Fancy, 43
Harlequin and the Forty Virgins, 82
Harlequin and his Seven Brothers, 59
Harlequin Jack and the Beanstalk, 67
Harlequin Little King Pippin, 56
Harlequin Oliver Cromwell, 32
Harlequin Robin Hood, 31
Harlequin and the Swans, 82
Harlequin Whittington, 43
Heartbreak House, 36
Hit or Miss, 83
Hunter of the Alps, The, 36, 68
Hyder Ali, 47

Illuminated Lake, The, 53
Infernal Secret, The, 100
Invasion of Russia, The, 43
Ivanhoe, 47

Jack Cade, 59
Jack the Giant-killer, 31
Jack Sheppard, 31, 32, 36, 80, 95

James Dance, or the Unfortunate Ship's Boy, 60
James Flaunty, or the Terror of the Western Seas, 60
John of Paris, 83
Jonathan Bradford, 56
Julius Cæsar, 53

King Arthur, 59
Korastikan, 47

La Perouse, 82
Life in London ("Tom and Jerry"), 42, 57, 80, 98
Life in Paris, 99
Life of a Soldier, The, 32
Lord Darnley, 31
Lord Mayor's Fool, The, 31, 57
Loves of Mars and Venus, 81

Macbeth, 79
Maid and the Magpie, The, 73, 74, 83
Mary, Maid of the Inn, 31, 55
Mazeppa, 59
Miller and his Men, The, 17, 19, 20, 22, 24, 28, 45, 53, 56, 59, 62, 64, 67, 68, 73, 74, 78, 79, 80, 83, 84, 85, 86, 88, 98
Montrose, or the Children of the Mist, 52
Mother Goose, 82
Mysterious Traveller, The, 60

Oliver Twist, 73, 80
Olympic Revels, 50, 80

Paul Clifford, 36, 73, 80
Pilot, The, 36, 46, 49, 50, 80
Pizarro, 82, 95, 96

Raymond and Agnes, or the Bleeding Nun, 53, 82
Red Rover, 36, 46, 78
Ride to York, The, 31
Rifle Volunteers, The, 68
Roadside Inn, The, 59
Robbers of the Rhine, The, 85
Robber's Wife, The, 83
Robin Hood, 64, 68
Robinson Crusoe, 59, 83
Rob Roy, 43
Romeo and Juliet, 52
Rookwood, 31

[117]

Scourge of the Gulph, The, 60
Secret Mine, The, 30, 35
Seven Wonders of the World, or Harlequin Colossus, 31
Silver Palace, The, 16
Sixteen-string Jack, 32
Skeleton Horseman, The, 59
Sleeping Beauty, The, 74
Smuggler, The, 36, 62
Spectre Bride, The, 53

Telemachus, 43
Therese, or The Orphan of Geneva, 31, 54
Three-fingered Jack, 36
Tiger's Hoard, The, 31
Timour the Tartar, 55, 74
Tom Daring, or Far from Home, 59
Tom and Jerry ("Life in London"), 42, 57, 80, 98

Treasure of the Garden, The, 60
Triumph of Neptune, The, 75
True to the Core, 78
Two Gentlemen of Verona, 43

Uncle Tom's Cabin, 80
Undine, 43
Union Jack, 68

Valentine and Orson, 82
Venice Preserv'd, 83

Waterman, The, 31, 57
Whittington and his Cat, 32, 102
Wild Boy, The, 42
Wood Demon, The, 53
Woodman's Hut, The, 101
Wreck Ashore, 31

DOLLS AND PUPPETS

By MAX von BOEHN. *Translated from the German by Josephine Nicoll, with a Note on Puppets by George Bernard Shaw. With 30 Plates in Colour and 464 other Illustrations. Demy 8vo. 30s. net.*

"I always hold up the wooden actors as instructive object-lessons to our flesh-and-blood players. The wooden ones... move you as only the most experienced living actors can." Thus G.B.S. places on record here his view of the importance of puppets, to the subject of which half this volume is devoted. The book is the first to give a connected history of both the doll and the marionette. It takes us back to prehistoric times, when naked savage children played with their dolls like any modern child, and to ancient Egypt and classical Greece, when the marionette show pleased as much as the Punch and Judy does to-day. It includes many diverse forms—the 'still-life' Nativity scene, the Chinese shadow-plays, and the puppets controlled by hand, rod, or string, as well as the most modern developments, such as Podrecca's famous Teatro dei Piccoli in Rome and the many remarkable puppet-shows of Germany. Nor does the author lose sight of larger movements in his treatment of the details; and the text is accompanied throughout by a magnificent gallery of illustrations. "This is an enchanted and enchanting land into which Herr von Boehn conducts us," commented *The Times Literary Supplement* in its review of the German edition, which has been here translated by the wife of Professor Allardyce Nicoll, herself an authority on the subject.

Daily Mail

NORTHCLIFFE HOUSE, LONDON, E.C.4.
Telephone: Central 6000.

2nd March, 1937. 61st Day.

The death, announced yesterday, of Mr. Walter Melville, elder of the famous Melville brothers, recalls the days when melodrama flourished at the Lyceum and many another London theatre.

What has become of those rich old shows which thrilled pre-war audiences? "To-day they would seem just a joke," says

CLIVE MacMANUS

'Daily Mail' Drama Critic

who in the article below recalls some of the famous thrillers of bygone days.

This was how it looked in the old days . . . at the Royal Victoria Theatre.

These Were Real Melodramas!

IS melodrama dead? Do Faces at the Window no longer frighten? Do Girls Who Lose Their Characters excite no pity from the gods? I fear so.

It is a disturbing thought, to those who loved the old melodramas, that these things have lost their pre-war popularity and that it is as much as ten years since Tod Slaughter froze our marrows at the Elephant—even if he is still doing it on the wireless and screen.

London has no home of melodrama now. Drury Lane no longer has its autumn drama, the Adelphi abandoned it years ago, the Surrey is no more. The Elephant, the Standard, Shoreditch (where the Melvilles made their London début), and the Britannia, Hoxton, something for your money. You saw things *happen* in their plays, and you could hear all the players, even if you were perched at the back of the gallery.

Drury Lane led the way with those stupendous autumn dramas, each of which held its own sensation. In early days this was created by two Maxim guns, one on each side of the stage, firing in a darkened theatre. That was in "A Life of Pleasure," and had no reference to life in Chicago.

Then there were real racehorses really racing on the revolving stage, as in "The Whip," real water, in a tank, for a more or less real submarine (in "The Price of Peace"), and real motor-cars.

What superb adventuresses were portrayed at the Lane by Mrs. Raleigh, and what noble-hearted comedians by George Barrett!

Then there was the Princess's, in Oxford-street, where, as a child, I can remember being taken across the stage Boucicault's Irish masterpieces, "The Colleen Bawn" and "The Shaughraun"; "The Octoroon," in which a beautiful near-white girl was put up for auction in the slave market.

"The Girl From the Jam Factory." "The Girl Without a Home" (*Save him and you condemn your father!*)

"A Girl's Good Luck," which introduced a real Tube train; "A Woman's Pluck" (introducing the Lady Boxer). "Was She To Blame?" (*Just as proud as you are of the name of clergyman am I of the name of actress!*) "The Female Detective" (*Go! But if he dies I will hunt you to your doom!*)

Will it Return?

WILL the vogue for melodrama ever return? I doubt it.

Sensation and sometimes spectacle find their place in the modern thriller; humour is all-important; but there is little room for sentimentality frighten? Do Girls Who Lose Their Characters excite no pity from the gods? I fear so.

It is a disturbing thought, to those who loved the old melodramas, that these things have lost their pre-war popularity and that it is as much as ten years since Tod Slaughter froze our marrows at the Elephant—even if he is still doing it on the wireless and screen.

London has no home of melodrama now. Drury Lane no longer has its autumn drama, the Adelphi abandoned it years ago, the Surrey is no more. The Elephant, the Standard, Shoreditch (where the Melvilles made their London début), and the Britannia, Hoxton,

Here is a playbill of the famous "East Lynne."

are cinemas. The West London, which lies somewhere near the Edgware-road, is, I am told, a warehouse.

The only plays in which "*music is introduced to heighten the emotional or dramatic effect*"—for that is the strict definition of melodrama—are Shakespearean productions and certain "highbrow" dramas in verse.

That striking combination of sensationalism, sob-stuff, and low comedy which delighted the old gods is found nowadays only in the cinemas. (There it loses its savour.

The days of melodrama were good days. They were good for audiences, actors, producers, and even authors.

Things "Happened"

THE late Andrew Melville, father of the Melville brothers, left £100,000; Mrs. Sara Lane, of the "Old Brit.," £125,000, and George Conquest, of the Surrey, £65,000—all the profits of melodrama and pantomime.

Of the authors, Henry Pettitt, associated with Drury Lane, left some £50,000. If George R. Sims and Cecil Raleigh left less they had in their time done pretty well with melodrama.

The purveyors of melodrama deserved to die rich, for they gave you

---

A COUNTRYMAN'S DIARY

March 1   *The Lamps of the Gorses*

THERE were many blossoms on the gorses, especially those that make shaggy the southern slope of the down, before the blizzard whited the land. And if there should be a streak of north in the wind for some days to come the flowers, though they will not increase, certainly will not become fewer. It seems as though the gorses were meant to keep some cheer under all conditions.

In the depth of winter, with frozen snow on the ground and every bush and tree stiff with frost, you may go out and count the handful of yellow blooms which were open when the ice-wind blew, and find them just the same day after day until a softer breeze stirs and the ice slips away. Set like little lamps in the frozen bushes, they shine on for a sign of what will follow the cold and desolate time.

PERCY W. D. IZZARD.

---

could hear all the players, even those who were perched at the back of the gallery.

Drury Lane led the way with those stupendous autumn dramas, each of which held its own sensation. In early days this was created by two Maxim guns, one on each side of the stage, firing in a darkened theatre. That was in "A Life of Pleasure," and had no reference to life in Chicago.

Then there were real racehorses really racing on the revolving stage, as in "The Whip," real water, in a tank, for a more or less real submarine (in "The Price of Peace"), and real motor-cars.

What superb adventuresses were portrayed at the Lane by Mrs. Raleigh, and what noble-hearted comedians by George Barrett!

Then there was the Princess's, in Oxford-street, where, as a child, I can remember being taken across the stage in a scene representing Henley Regatta (with real water) in "The Dark Secret."

I remember sitting in the wings at the Standard, Shoreditch, while "The Girl Who Lost Her Character" was in process of smashing every piece of crockery within her reach on the stage, and the stage manager was busy shaking a bucket full of real crockery to provide the sound which the plaster-of-paris ware failed to give out.

Women With Daggers

I HAVE wept at the death of Miss Haidée Wright as one of "Two Little Vagabonds"; shuddered at Charles Warner staggering in "Drink," jumped in my seat as two women (in *full* evening dress) battled with daggers in "Women and Wine."

I have seen heroines saved from saw-mills, midnight expresses, fires (by acrobats on the telegraph wires), weirs, and wickedness.

The very names of these old plays stir the blood. The catchwords on the posters, too. Who could forget them?

"*Dead—and never lived to call me Mother.*" Sad, that the most moving moment in "East Lynne" should live only as a music-hall joke.

Those melodramas were varied enough—"The Ticket-of-Leave Man," with Hawkshaw the Detective; Dion

---

Are Men So Childlike?

To the Editor of "The Daily Mail"

SIR,—I am a spinster, nearly 23. I have had three proposals of marriage, but as yet have not been able to say "Yes." There appears to me to be a great strain of unreliability in the men I meet, and in many cases they are ill mannered.

A woman likes someone on whom she can depend. Only one man in my short but full experience has kept an appointment absolutely to time.

A woman looks on man as a child. He may resent it, but generally her attitude is justified.   S. J.

Petersham.

Serial Dreams

SIR,—I have read the accounts by correspondents of their prophetic dreams. I, too, have these, but I have also experienced something which is, I believe, equally as unusual—serial dreams.

Every night, for perhaps a week, I dream an instalment of an exciting drama.

On each succeeding night my mind picks up the thread of the story from the dream of the previous night.

I'm just an ordinary modern girl, and do not consider myself "psychic" in any way

Farnham, Surrey.   C.

Temperamental Cats

SIR,—I possess a large, beautiful black cat, a male of two years old, whose emotions toward me are obviously as changeable as the wind.

He has fits of alternating indifference,

---

beautiful near-white girl was put up for auction in the slave market.

"The Girl From the Jam Factory." "The Girl Without a Home" (*Save him and you condemn your father!*)

"A Girl's Good Luck," which introduced a real Tube train; "A Woman's Pluck" (introducing the Lady Boxer). "Was She To Blame?" (*Just as proud as you are of the name of clergyman am I of the name of actress!*) "The Female Detective" (*Go! But if he dies I will hunt you to your doom!*)

Will it Return?

WILL the vogue for melodrama ever return? I doubt it.

Sensation and sometimes spectacle find their place in the modern thriller; humour is all-important; but there is little room for sentimentality.

Even virtue is not always triumphant nowadays; consider "The Amazing Dr. Clitterhouse," who gets away with murder.

Loudspeakers are sometimes used to "heighten the effect," as in "The Frog," but stage children die no more to soft music and murders are not now heralded by a feverish strumming of violin strings.

It is not only the realism of the films that has killed melodrama. The modern theatre audience knows too much to be moved by the frenzied emotions that stirred their ancestors or to be dazzled by the stage lights of London.

Long London runs were not as a rule enjoyed by the old melodramas. Their real life was the tour from town to town in the provinces. Such plays as "The Grip of Iron," "The Face at the Window," and "The Worst Woman in London" moved for years round the Kingdom, always delighting fresh audiences.

The War struck the first blow at the touring melodrama company. The cinema struck the second. The sharpness of a more sophisticated and experienced generation has virtually given it the knock-out.

There may be places here and there where its devotees still gather; but for most people Melodrama to-day is just one great big beautiful Joke.

---

toleration, and ardent affection, which make me wonder if he is different from other cats or whether they are all so fickle.

I have recently acquired a puppy, and notice that the cat now eats twice as much as he did when he was the only pet of the house.   (Mrs.) J. SPOONER.

Rugby-road, Wallasey.

Where To Retire

SIR,—Your correspondents, in grading the affability of various counties, have taken them from the casual tourists' angle.

Can they suggest a likely place for residents of moderate means to retire permanently—a district where simple hospitality is given and offered, and a hand is extended to welcome those who are not bridge or golf players?   L. D.

Pontrug, Caernarvon.

A White Blackbird

SIR,—For more than two years now we in this little village of Craster in North Northumberland have had with us a white blackbird.

These winter days, as he perches on the leafless and almost black branches, he makes an interesting nature study in black and white.

Unlike the blackbirds mentioned by Alan Bell in his recent nature article, with their "magical golden notes," this one has never been heard to sing.

He is all white with a yellow beak, is very timid, and is often seen with a blackbird of "regulation colours."   E. A.

Church-st., Craster, Alnwick.

...by much at a handicap... hang over the hurdle in an agony suspense.

...e competition is fierce, and there probably never been more beautiful figure-skating seen anywhere than ...rl's Court yesterday morning and ...rnoon.

...iting Their Turn

...great rink is divided into three ... On one the examination is in ...ress. On the next eight men with ...ms and one with a hose prepare ...ice for the next fine etching of ...rns.

On the third, the girls who are waiting their turn glide, turn, lunge, and whirl in ceaseless busy practice.

...ey are a colourful crowd of ...gsters, all aged 18 or less, all ...tly and differently dressed.

...ss Colledge, as usual, is sombre ... discreet in a short dress of fine ... wool. She practises in scarlet ...g gloves and wears white ones ...ng her tense few minutes before ...udges. She wears no jewellery; ...ead is bare.

...riotic Colours

...ss Megan Taylor, in a patriotic ...t of red, white and blue, skims ...d the rink in a white jersey dress ... red and blue frills at wrist and ... tricoloured bandeau, white boots ...gloves.

...ss Vivi-Anne Hulten, her nearest ..., is one of the three competitors ...hallenge attention by being dressed ...rely in scarlet.

...ss Martha Mayerhans, one of the ...nan competitors, and Miss Hedy ...uf, the French champion, are both ...carlet, too.

...ll-Cap

...ss Viktoria Lindpaintner, the ...nan champion, is one of the best ...ok at. She is a big girl with dark, ... hair, a plump, attractive face, ...very long legs. She wears a ...ng dress and skull-cap of mid-...t-blue velvet.

...ss Belita Jepson-Turner, the Eng-...competitor, aged 13, is the most ...acularly dressed—all in white. **She skates with the grace of a ...list dancer (she is one) and ...ishes with a little half-pirouette ...at has nothing in common with ... neat, reserved "coming-to-rest" Miss Colledge and the others.**

...ss Audrey Peppe (pronounced ...y), the tiny American champion, ... 18, has an almost comical non-...ance on the ice which is amusing ...atch.

With it—and Why?

CAPT. FRANK H. SHAW—expert on ships and shippers, crews and cargoes—discusses the somewhat painful problem of British mercantile shipping.

In the process of explaining where we have gone wrong, he hints, very practically, at how we might yet evolve a policy that would mean prosperity.

His article will interest all whose "She" is a ship; it appears to-day in the London

EVENING NEWS

Huge Bets on 3 Cup Favourites

By ARBITER

"I'LL take three monkeys to one (£1,500 to £500) about the Arsenal for the Cup," a leading bookmaker said yesterday. The best odds he was offered were 11-4.

I knew there was a good deal of betting on the Football Association Cup competition among professional racing people, but I was surprised to learn that it was on this huge scale.

Among the chief bets yesterday were £600 to £200 against the Arsenal and £450 to £100 against Manchester City.

The chief operator is a Midland bookmaker, who first backs the teams and then lays them off at reduced prices.

Most of the big money has gone on the Arsenal, Manchester City, and Wolverhampton Wanderers, and the prices offered against them yesterday, together with the other clubs to take part in next Saturday's ties, were:—

**11-4 Arsenal.
4-1 Manchester City.
9-2 Wolverhampton Wanderers.
7-1 Sunderland.
9-1 Preston North End and West Bromwich Albion.
10-1 Tottenham Hotspur; and
20-1 Millwall.**

. Arbiter's review of the Cup prospects is in Page 18.

8,000,000 Wireless Licences

TO-DAY'S WEATHER
(Forecast in Page 15)
Showers

...AR AND NEAR

MAJOR TRYON stated in the House of Commons yesterday that the number of wireless ...ving licences in force on January 31 was 8,071,464, compared with ...131 last November.

...itain's latest destroyer, H.M.S. ...lsive, was launched at Cowes yesterday.

...solicitor's clerk, Mr. Harry ..., of Chipstead-way, Woodmansterne, Surrey, collapsed and died at ...aw Courts yesterday.

...hschild Treasures.—The contents ... late Lord and Lady Rothschild's ... at 148, Piccadilly, including ...art treasures, will be sold at ...eby's next month.

...mbria Returns.—The Imperial ...ys flying-boat Cambria re-...d to Southampton yesterday from ...ew Atlantic airport on the River ...non, where she had been making ...ghts.

...ygen Tents for Hire.—A new and ...ved type of oxygen tent is ...ut on hire. It was announced at ...pening of the Nursing Exhibition ...ndon yesterday.

...dge Indisposed—Derby Assizes ...g to the indisposition of Mr. Jus-...Humphreys, who is 60, and he will ...resume duty until Thursday.

H.M.S. VALIANT, the battleship which recently returned to Devonport from the Mediterranean, was yesterday transferred to dockyard control to begin a refit which will cost about £1,000,000 and occupy two years.

Tube Extension.—London Transport yesterday placed a £650,000 contract for boring tunnels between Liverpool-street and Mile End.

Crystal Palace trustees yesterday considered tenders for the ruins left from the fire, but it was stated that no decision would be taken until next Monday.

Fire Destroys Mansion.—Furniture which had been in the family of Mr. John Hurd, squire of Nettleham, for generations, was lost when Nettleham Hall, near Lincoln, was destroyed by fire yesterday.

18 Years at No. 10.—Mr W. H. P...er, on retiring after 18 years at No. 10 Downing-street—the last six as office keeper—has received a gold watch from the staff and gold cufflinks from Mrs. Baldwin.

OBITUARY

Deaths announced include:
Mr. De Witt Jennings, the United States film actor who played in "Mutiny on the Bounty" and "Trial of Mary Dugan"; at Hollywood, aged 5?.

The National Hunt meeting at Cheltenham—the Ascot of winter racing—was postponed for a week owing to heavy rain, while snow caused the cancellation of the Quorn and Fernie Hunt meets.

The death roll in the storm now amounts to 13.

Sleighs Bring Milk

Horse-drawn Sleighs brought the milk to Princetown, Dartmoor.

Missing Barge.—A message was broadcast to ships last night asking them to keep a look-out for the motor barge Airston, which left Fingringhoe, Essex, on Saturday with a crew of three, and is believed to have sunk off West Maplin Spit, Shoeburyness. A wreck has been seen at this spot.

Fishing Boat Wrecked.—The fishing boat Jane and William was pounded to pieces when driven on the rocks at Dunbar, East Lothian, but the crew of three escaped.

Collapsed in Snow.—Exhausted by her struggles through deep drifts, Miss Beatrice Beedle, aged 33, collapsed in the snow at New Deer, Aberdeenshire, and died from exposure.

Four Children Orphaned.—By the death of Walter Henry Roberts, of Eyton, near Wrexham, from injuries received in a road accident on Sunday

"WORLD'S LOVELIEST EYES" IN COURT CASE

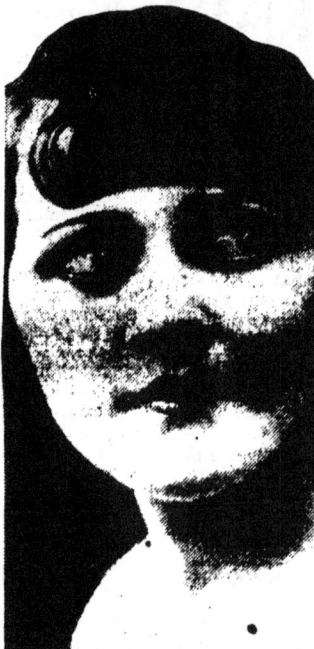

A portrait by wire from Paris last night of Mlle. Mado Taylor, the "woman with the world's most beautiful eyes." Yesterday she gave evidence in the Paris law courts with one of them bandaged—as a result, she alleged, of a blow aimed by a man who "insulted" her because she "occupied the pavement" while sheltering with a friend under an umbrella. He was fined £10.

four children are orphaned. Mrs. Roberts was killed in the smash.

Death on Rescue Bid.—Mr. William Taylor, aged 70, an engineer, of Mowsley, Leicestershire, set out to help his son, whose car was stranded in a drift, and did not return. A search party found him lying dead a short distance from his home.

LINER RESCUES CREW

Unusually high tides caused widespread flooding in Venice, and gondolas were floating in St. Mark's-square.

The Anchor liner Tuscania arrived at Gibraltar, bringing the captain and 16 members of the crew of the Italian steamer Yolanda which sprang a leak and sank off Cadiz early yesterday. One member of the crew was drowned.

...spect of singing with T... playing again in London ... forgotten to ask what the rôle, is about—or even ... am to get," she told a reporter.

Her husband, Mr. Fran... with her. He says that part comes along he m... again on the West End ...

MR. John Gielg... production of "... which he played the ti... a record run on Broadw...

He's Tired Of Being Hamlet

He decl... tired of p... for it was strain. M... ran 132 ni... way and th... provinces. There is n... Americans are excellent ... Shakespeare, but I thi... British productions best.

Mr. Edmund Gwenn, t... who has made four pict... wood, is going to tak... costume play—about Sam... London.

MRS. Natalie Kain... director of Technic... has come over to su... filming of the Coronation British Movietone News.

" Besides the actual ceremony," she said, " we shall also take ' shots ' of the Crown Jewels, the Tower of London, and other historic items. We... cial process for portray... the only thing I am r... about is the weather. I ... sunshine."

AS for the Queen M... she is now—in t... her commander, Capt... her crew and her pa...

"The Perfect Ship"

near as po... fect ship."
Though through from Amb... Cherbourg 14hrs., at an average of... alterations made durin... lay-up have worked wo... "There has been con... rolling, despite heavy s... Capt. Peel, "and vibrat... practically eliminated."

Negus's Inv...

Replying in the Ho... mons yesterday to Mr. ... (C., Torquay), who as... invitation was sent to the represented at the Cor... Eden said :

" The invitations we... accordance with precede... based entirely on the de... It would be a mistak... special political significa... ter of purely normal proc...

THE DUKE OF

From Our Own Corr...
MUNIC...

The Duke of Kent, w... staying with the Duke ... Enzesfeld, arrived here ... Venna.

The Duke and Duchess ... Munich for a few days, ... they are expected to go t...

FELL UNDER

Alfred Gale, aged 14, ... Dagenham, Essex, fell ... platform and an elect... Becontree railway statio... and crawled out from un... laughing and unhurt.

The electric current ... turned off before the boy ... move and the service wa... 15 minutes.

NOEL COWAR...

From Our Own Corr...
NEW YOR...

The... of Noel Co... suffering from laryngit... week's break at the r... To-night at 8.30, w... drawing crowded hous... last November.

Daily Mail

NORTHCLIFFE HOUSE, LONDON, E.C.4.
Telephone: Central 6000.

2nd March, 1937. 61st Day.

The death, announced yesterday, of Mr. Walter Melville, elder of the famous Melville brothers, recalls the days when melodrama

That striking combination of sensationalism, sob-stuff, and low comedy which delighted the old gods is found nowadays only in the cinemas. There it loses its savour.

The days of melodrama were good days. They were good for audiences, actors, producers, and even authors.

Things "Happened"

THE late Andrew Melville, father of the Melville brothers, left £100,000; Mrs. Sara Lane, of the "Old Brit.," £125,000, and George Conquest, of the Surrey, £65,000—all the profits of melodrama and pantomime.

Of the authors, Henry Pettitt, associated with Drury Lane, left some £50,000. If George R. Sims and Cecil Raleigh left less they had in their time done pretty well with melodrama.

The purveyors of melodrama deserved to die rich, for they gave you Mother." Sad, that the most moving moment in "East Lynne" should live only as a music-hall joke.

Those melodramas were varied enough—"The Ticket-of-Leave Man," with Hawkshaw the Detective; Dion cated and experienced generation has virtually given it the knock-out.

There may be places here and there where its devotees still gather; but for most people Melodrama to-day is just one great big beautiful Joke.

A Countryman's Diary

March 1   *The Lamps of the Gorses*

THERE were many blossoms on the gorses, especially those that make shaggy the southern slope of the down, before the blizzard whited the land. And if there should be a streak of north in the wind for some days to come the flowers, though they will not increase, certainly will not become fewer. It seems as though the gorses were meant to keep some cheer under all conditions.

In the depth of winter, with frozen snow on the ground and every bush and tree stiff with frost, you may go out and count the handful of yellow blooms which were open when the ice-wind blew, and find them just the same day after day until a softer breeze stirs and the ice slips away. Set like little lamps in the frozen bushes, they shine on for a sign of what will follow the cold and desolate time.

PERCY W. D. IZZARD.

Are Men So Childlike?

To the Editor of "The Daily Mail"

SIR,—I am a spinster, nearly 23. I have had three proposals of marriage, but as yet have not been able to say "Yes." There appears to me to be a great strain of unreliability in the men I meet, and in many cases they are ill mannered.

A woman likes someone on whom she can depend. Only one man in my short but full experience has kept an appointment absolutely to time.

A woman looks on man as a child. He may resent it, but generally her attitude is justified.   S. J.

Petersham.

Serial Dreams

SIR,—I have read the accounts by correspondents of their prophetic dreams. I, too, have these, but I have also experienced something which is, I believe, equally as unusual—serial dreams.

Every night, for perhaps a week, I dream an instalment of an exciting drama.

On each succeeding night my mind picks up the thread of the story from the dream of the previous night.

I'm just an ordinary modern girl, and do not consider myself "psychic" in any way.

Farnham, Surrey.   C.

Temperamental Cats

SIR,—I possess a large, beautiful black cat, a male of two years old, whose emotions toward me are obviously as changeable as the wind.

He has fits of alternating indifference, toleration, and ardent affection, which make me wonder if he is different from other cats or whether they are all so fickle.

I have recently acquired a puppy, and notice that the cat now eats twice as much as he did when he was the only pet of the house.   (Mrs.) J. SPOONER.

Rugby-road, Wallasey.

Where To Retire

SIR,—Your correspondents, in grading the affability of various counties, have taken them from the casual tourists' angle.

Can they suggest a likely place for residents of moderate means to retire permanently—a district where simple hospitality is given and offered, and a hand is extended to welcome those who are not bridge or golf players?   L. D.

Pontrug, Caernarvon.

A White Blackbird

SIR,—For more than two years now we in this little village of Craster in North Northumberland have had with us a white blackbird.

These winter days, as he perches on the leafless and almost black branches, he makes an interesting nature study in black and white.

Unlike the blackbirds mentioned by Alan Bell in his recent nature article, with their "magical golden notes," this one has never been heard to sing.

He is all white with a yellow beak; is very timid, and is often seen with a blackbird of "regulation colours."   E. A.

Church-st., Craster, Alnwick.

www.ingramcontent.com/pod-product-compliance
Lightning Source LLC
LaVergne TN
LVHW061308060426
835507LV00019B/2069